THE LITTLE BOOK OF

Whisky

Thierry Bénitah

Flammarion

Q U E S T I O N S

Walk into a store selling whisky anywhere and you will find a vast array of blends, single malts, and bourbons. This complex world of flavors takes time to explore, but is rich in rewards. What are the characteristics of each type of whisky?

Whisky-making is an ancient tradition, but is the place of the traditional distilleries being challenged by newcomers to the scene like Japan, which now offers quality whiskies of its own? What part do heritage and tradition play in the creation of a fine whisky?

Some connoisseurs will only drink whisky from one distillery, even from one particular barrel. What is the most important factor in choosing a good whisky? Is age to be prized over country of origin?

A N S W E R S

Orientation p. 6

The alphabetical entries have been classified according to the following categories. Each category is indicated with a small colored square.

■ The Product: ■ Production: ▢ Context:
  Origins   Distilling   History
  Varieties   Tasting   Trade
                  Whisky Drinkers

The information given in each entry, together with cross-references indicated by asterisks, enables the reader to explore the world of whisky.

The Story of Whisky p. 10

The Story of Whisky provides a detailed overview of the themes and information provided in the alphabetical entries.

Alphabetical Guide p. 28

The entries, arranged in alphabetical order, tell you all you need to know to find your way around this fascinating world. The information is enriched with detailed discussion of all the major whisky-producing countries and text boxes which highlight specific elements of whisky production.

O R I E N T A T I O N

I. THE STORY OF WHISKY

A. An Eventful History

The story of whisky is a story of struggle: national claims to the invention of the golden drink, the eternal conflict between distillers and the exciseman, the temperance brigade's efforts against drunkenness, and, last but not least, the commercial rivalry that, happily, has led to ever better whiskies.

- *Bootlegger*
- ■ *Bushmills*
- *Clan*
- *DCL*
- ■ *Glenlivet*
- *License*
- ■ *Midleton*
- *Poteen*
- *Prohibition*
- *Uisge Beatha*

B. The Men who Made Whisky

Whisky claims Saint Patrick as its inventor—a story based more in legend than in truth. The true history of whisky has been influenced by all sorts of men, from eccentric priests to ingenious inventors, from bold smugglers to inspired poets, all of whom have left their mark.

- *Burns (Robert)*
- *Coffey (Aeneas)*
- *Craig (Elijah)*
- ■ *Daniel (Jack)*
- *Eunson (Magnus)*
- ■ *Jameson (John)*
- *Lloyd George (David)*
- *Power (John)*
- *Saint Patrick*
- *Usher (Andrew)*
- *Walker (Hiram)*

C. The Whisky Trade

Today, whisky is sold and enjoyed all over the planet, and its popularity knows no bounds. For many countries, it is a major source of income, in terms of export revenue or as a taxed luxury. And indeed whisky is one of life's luxuries: its subtle charms require an educated palate, which can take a lifetime to acquire.

- *Consumption*
- *Independent bottler*
- *Preservation*
- *Specialist*
- *Tax*

II. THE AUTHENTICITY OF WHISKY

A. The Whisky Countries

Whether the credit for its invention goes to the Irish or the Scots, whisky is deeply rooted in both cultures. Today, other nations associated with whisky are the United States, Canada, and even Japan.

- *Canada*
- *Ireland*
- *Japan*
- *Scotland*
- *United States*

B. Whisky Production

Today, distilling is a thoroughly modern industry, yet it keeps some of the romanticism of its past, when there was a touch of magic in the proceedings. The four elements—water, earth, air, and fire—combine to transform basic ingredients into something extraordinary.

- *Aging*
- *Blending*
- *Casks*
- *Distillation*
- *Fermentation*
- *Grain*
- *Kiln*
- *Label*
- *Liqueur*
- *Malting*
- *Manufacture*
- *Mashing*
- *Peat*
- *Still*
- *Water*

C. Whisky Regions

Certain whisky lovers can tell exactly which distillery a whisky comes from, and even the year of bottling. Each region has its own characteristic and distinctive taste, and each has its particular admirers.

- *Campbeltown*
- *Highlands*
- *Islay*
- *Kentucky*
- *Lowlands*
- *Speyside*
- *Tennessee*

III. A PASSION FOR WHISKY

A. Whisky Tasting

Tasting is an especially delicate art when it comes to whisky, as the tastes and aromas offered by each different whisky show an astonishing and subtle range of variations. There are some rules, however, to guide you in your choice.

- Age
- Aroma
- Club
- Color
- Combination
- Glasses
- Label
- Taste
- Tasting

B. The Image of Whisky

Heart-warming remedy to cheat a cold, or insidious poison destroying the drinker? Whisky has been both of these. Fortunately, today's drinkers tend to be less extreme, and appreciate a "wee dram" for its flavor. Of course, whisky plays a leading role in many a film and book.

- Collecting
- Liqueur
- Literature and Cinema
- Medicinal
- Packaging
- Sociability
- Spirits
- Vocabulary

C. Choosing a Whisky

Connoisseurs do not just order a whisky—they choose a Scotch, bourbon, single malt, or blend, according to their mood. Here are some key points to help you find your way through the maze of whiskies available.

- Blend
- Bourbon
- Cask strength
- Grain (single)
- Malt
- Rye
- Scotch
- Single cask
- Single malt
- Sour mash
- Whiskey

THE STORY OF WHISKY

Whisky drinkers are a breed apart: the drink's charms can take some getting used to, and it requires a refined palate to appreciate a good dram to the full. However, the pleasures of sipping a really fine whisky by the fire after a long walk in the cold are a worthy reward for anyone patient enough to become a true connoisseur.

I. The adventure of whisky
A. An eventful history

Whisky (from the Gaelic *uisge beatha**, meaning "water of life") is a very old drink, and history has not always been in its favor. The most striking development in the twentieth century was the enormous reduction in the number of whisky distilleries. This sad fact is true for all whisky-producing countries, foremost among them Scotland, Ireland, and the United States. In the United States, the scale of the disappearance of traditional distilleries can justifiably be described as catastrophic. At the close of the nineteenth century, the high point of American whiskey production, there were 780 distilleries in the United States: 350 of these were in North Carolina, 172 in Kentucky, 72 in Georgia, 62 in Pennsylvania, 51 in Virginia, 47 in Tennessee, and there were even a few distilleries to be found in Alabama and California. Today, only twelve of these survive. Scotland and Ireland have both suffered similar losses. In 1996, for example, there remained only three distilleries in Ireland as compared to twenty-eight a hundred years earlier. Scotland has seen the number of its distilleries fall from 170 in 1880 to about one hundred today, of which only eighty are still productive. The last ten years have even witnessed an acceleration in closures.

There is some hope for the future, however. Some new sites have opened. Among them is a malt distillery that began operating in 1996 on the Isle of Aran, in the Western Lowlands of Scotland. There are several factors behind the whisky industry's difficulties, but both producers and sellers agree that their trade has been bedevilled by two problems since it began: the fight against alcoholism, and heavy taxes. Back in the olden days, the first taxes on whisky meant more and more people began to distill their own illicit whisky (known as poteen* in Ireland). The modern version of the whisky smuggler, the bootlegger*, was kept busy during Prohibition* in 1930s America. In the Scottish Highlands of the eighteenth century, the different clans saw illicit distilling as a political gesture against English rule.

Happily, the history of whisky has not always been such a troubled business. Some outstanding figures are remembered with fondness to this day for their contribution to the whisky story. But the battle for supremacy in the world of whisky continues: Scotch seems to be the winner today, but Irish whiskey and American bourbon have surely not said their last word.

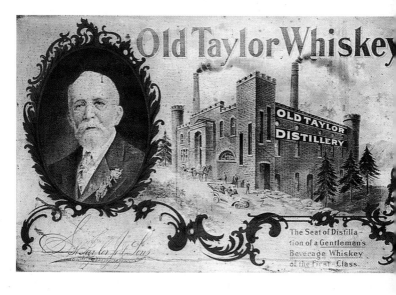

The Seat of Distillation of a Gentleman's Beverage Whiskey of the First-Class.

Label for the Old Taylor brand.

B. The men who made whisky

Whisky owes a great deal of its enduring popularity as a drink to a few inspired men, both distillers and businessmen. For some of these heroes, it is hard to separate the myth from reality: the history books say whisky appeared in Ireland some five hundred years ago; some die-hard traditionalists swear that the earliest *uisge beatha**** was made by the fifth-century Irish monks who brought the secret of distilling from the Middle East; the Irish themselves see their patron saint, Saint Patrick*, as the father of whisky (although there is no historical proof to back this up); the Scots simply smile and point out that Saint Patrick was born—in Scotland. Fifteen hundred years later, another monk, Magnus Eunson*, showed by his bold smuggling exploits how far the Scots will go for their national nectar.

The United States have their own "patron saint" of whisky—the Reverend Elijah Craig*, said to have invented bourbon. Other important, and less contested, figures in the history of whisky are Aeneas Coffey*, an inventor of genius, who gave his name to the patent still*, which led to Scotland's domination of the world of whisky. Scotland can also be grateful to Andrew Usher* who created the first quality blends* using the patent still. Some distillers have also gone down in history as men of foresight and conviction who built commercial empires that survive to the present day. In Ireland, John Power* and John Jameson are remembered in the famous brands named after them. Jack Daniel* in Tennessee made his brand the best-known bourbon in America. Hiram Walker* did the same in Canada. Whisky has always aroused passions: Scotland's national poet Robert Burns* sang its praises; British Prime Minister David Lloyd George* subdued the distillers with fierce penalties.

C. The whisky trade

Whisky began to be marketed commercially on a grand scale in the middle of the nineteenth century. Up until then, production had been divided between a few official distilleries and many illicit ones, whose produce was almost exclusively for local consumption. The development of reliable transport systems—particularly trains—during the Industrial Revolution meant whisky could travel further afield, and a few Scottish and Irish traders seized the golden opportunity to begin exporting their output.

Until 1945, production and consumption* were very much dependent on the rate of taxation* and the state of the world economy: it naturally fell during times of crisis. During the Second World War, production was virtually nil, but after 1945 it began to grow again, and indeed demand rose so rapidly that it far outstripped the production capacities of the distilleries. Scotland responded best to the challenge. By enlarging and modernizing its distilleries, it was able to dominate the market in Europe and America. In 1966, Irish whiskey producers fought back against this Scottish domination by grouping all Irish distilleries under the name Irish Distillers. Again, after the war, the Americans took advantage of their position to develop their whiskey export trade: to this day, the Japanese and German taste for the drink is said to be due to the presence of American GIs in their countries after 1945.

II. The authenticity of whisky
A. The whisky countries

Whisky immediately brings four countries to mind: Scotland*, Ireland*, the United States*, and Canada*. Where does their taste for whisky—or rather whiskies—come from? Part of the answer lies in the common heritage of the four countries. It seems it was the

Irish who invented whisky: they certainly introduced the art of distilling to Scotland. In the early sixteenth century, fleeing famine and persecution, Scottish and Irish families emigrated to North America, taking their precious recipes and stills with them. Eventually whisky-making spread all over the United States and Canada. For many, if not most, whisky lovers, whisky from any country other than these four is not worthy of the name.

There is, however, one other nation with a strong tradition of distilling alcoholic drinks: Japan*. Japanese involvement in the whisky industry dates from 1920, when Masataka Taketsuru, father of Japanese whisky, brought the secrets of whisky production back from Scotland, and adapted them to the climate and tastes of his homeland. Whisky experts consider Japanese brands to be fully deserving of respect, their particularity of style adding to their charm.

Not every country that makes whisky is admitted to the company of the greats. Wales, for instance, tries to legitimize its title by claiming for its own the father of whisky in a certain Reauilt Hir, who, they assert, pipped Saint Patrick to the post in the year 356. But the reason why Welsh brands do not figure among the cream of whiskies has nothing to do with history, and everything to do with taste. Unlike Scotch*, Irish whiskey*, and varieties from the other three countries, Welsh whisky has no special characteristics to distinguish it from the common herd. It is produced on similar lines to blended* Scottish whisky and has nothing to raise it above the average productions of other countries.

Irish, American, Canadian, and Japanese whiskies, on the other hand, are distinctive,

Italian caricature on the start of Prohibition, La Domenica del Corriere, 1919.

15

Daniel
Sherrin
(1895–1915).
*Highland
Landscape.*
London,
Christopher
Wood
Gallery.

each having its own particular characteristics, which mean that any-one can learn to tell them from Scotch with a bit of training. The range of flavors varies from brand to brand, each developing its own unique signature on the palate.

B. Whisky production

The principal ingredients of whisky are water* and grain*. Yeast may be added to encourage and control the process of fermentation. The flavor and aroma of a whisky are determined by the quality of the water (soft or hard; peaty or not) and the types of grain used (barley, corn, rye, wheat, or oats). As well as encouraging fermentation, the

yeast can also play a role in the flavor, imparting a hint of red fruits. The production* process differs slightly from whisky to whisky, but is always in five main stages: malting* (replaced by "cooking" in the United States), brewing*, fermentation*, distilling*, and aging*. In Scotland, peat* is introduced during the malting process, giving that characteristic "peaty" taste. It is used as a fuel in the kilns, and is also used occasionally in Irish whiskeys. In the United States, the first stage in whisky-making is called "cooking," and involves steaming a mixture of grains called "mashbill." Otherwise, the process is basically the same from country to country, except where distillation is concerned. In Scotland, malt whiskies are produced by a double

Following double page: fermentation at the Lagavulin Distillery. Isle of Islay, Scotland.

Spreading barley, Scotland.

distillation in "pot stills" where the process is not continuous. The opposite occurs in the case of grain alcohol, the other ingredient of blended whiskies, produced using Coffey's patent still for continuous distillation. This type of still is used in the United States and Canada.

Whatever the production process, the last stage is always aging in oak casks* which gives the whisky its final color, and its range of aromas and flavors.

C. Whisky regions

Just as wine drinkers can tell which region a particular wine comes from by its flavor, so the geography and climate of each whisky-producing region give a different taste and aroma to its products. The Scots claim that their whisky could not be produced anywhere

but in Scotland. What is more, every single Scottish brand has its own distinct characteristics. Take the example of the Lagavulin Distillery, which was established to imitate the product of its rival Laphroiag, a mere stone's throw away: despite using water from the same spring, the two drinks are quite different. Borrowing the notion of *terroir* from the world of wine, it is clear that geography has a vital role to play in the production of a fine whisky. This is why blends* are often only second choice for the connoisseur, as the characteristics of the different localities are lost in the blending process. Only malts* can truly claim to belong to a particular region. The notion is really only used in relation to Scotland with its hundred distilleries, and to a lesser degree in the United States, not in Ireland, Canada or Japan, as they have far fewer distilleries.

Single malts* and some American straight whiskeys rely on this idea of *terroir* for their individuality. Scottish whisky production is generally divided according to four geographic regions: the Lowlands*, Campbeltown*, Islay*, and the Highlands*. The Highlands are further subdivided into five regions: Speyside* in the center, and then the Northern, Eastern, Southern, and Western Highlands. The United States applies the same system, on a smaller scale. It is generally recognized that the two main producing states, Kentucky and Tennessee, have the clear advantage over the others in terms of water quality, the richness of their chalky soil, and their climate which is good for aging in casks. Each state also has its own production methods, which give distinctive characteristics to each whisky and allow tasters to build up a profile of each region.

III. A passion for whisky
A. Whisky tasting

Tasting* is a particularly delicate art when it comes to whisky, as each glass offers such a range of complex flavors* and aromas*. The best place to start is the label* on the bottle, which gives details of the origin, age*, alcoholic strength, and even type of cask used. However, it is wise not to stop at the label, and to look for further evidence inside the bottle. What about the color? The palette of shades available, from palest yellow to rich golden honey tones, gives a clue to the richness of the world of whisky. Yet color is not enough in itself to judge a whisky, since it can change considerably from one bottle to another of the same brand. Of course, the real proof of the pudding is in the drinking, using a proper whisky tumbler* designed to release the full flavor and aroma of the drink.

The basics of whisky tasting are easy to grasp, but the finer points can take a lifetime. You need not learn alone, though. Many clubs* have been set up to provide enthusiasts with the opportunity to taste many different whiskies, as individuals tend to stick to tried and trusted brands, thereby missing out on some treasures. It is often worthwhile joining one of these to meet fellow devotees and exchange experiences and tips.

Chivas whisky casks at the Glenlivet Distillery. Keith, Speyside, Scotland.

B. The image of whisky

Up until fairly recently, whisky was looked upon as a luxury. Over the last few years, however, it has become more widely available thanks to the development of chains of large retail stores, and although it is still not cheap, it is certainly more affordable than it

Preceding double page: Howard da Silva and Ray Milland enjoy a glass in *The Lost Weekend*, 1945.

was a few years ago. Historically, the image of whisky has changed a great deal over the centuries. In the sixteenth century, it was considered to have medicinal* properties (a notion which persists in the hot toddy to stave off colds and influenza). Today, the general tendency is to consider it a social evil, like tobacco. It is true that the image of whisky given in films and literature* has not always been very objective: from whisky-smugglers under Prohibition to hard-boiled private detectives swigging bourbon, whisky has been portrayed as a drink that leads to trouble.

Harry Eliot, *The Game of Chess*. Engraving, late nineteenth century, England.

Whisky producers today are attempting to change all that. Their advertising highlights the traditional nature of the drink and its "authentic," old-fashioned production methods, and, particularly associates Scotch with the history and heritage of a whole country (witness the many advertisements featuring wild, craggy mountain scenery and ruins of castles). The world of whisky is opening up. The technical vocabulary* of the specialist taster is filtering down to the general public, who are becoming more and more demanding about the quality of their drink. In particular, more and more women are learning to enjoy a "wee dram," where before they might have stuck to a more refined, smoother whisky-based liqueur*. Again, the manufacturers are picking up on these trends, and now issue special "limited edition" whiskies and packaging* for collectors*.

C. Choosing a whisky

For the whisky lover, the choice of dram is crucial. The best guide, as ever, is personal preference. Taste is at the top of the list. There are four basic taste families: salt, sweet, acid, and bitter. Each whisky has a particular permutation of these four categories that make up its own particular flavor. A bourbon* or Tennessee* whiskey will appeal to those who prefer a taste leaning towards sweetness, somewhere between caramel and vanilla. A rye* whiskey, on the other hand, is a subtle blend of sweet and bitter tastes.

Another reason to choose one whisky over another is the time of day when you will be enjoying your glass. The flavor of a whisky changes subtly as the day goes by. For instance, cask strength* whiskies and certain single casks* (or single barrels) have a very pronounced taste and are therefore not usually recommended as an apéritif. Blends*, straight or on the rocks, are better before a meal.

Scotch single malts* provide a huge range of aromas and flavors. Here, the choice is enormous. Novices are best advised to begin their training with a light whisky such as a Lowlands malt, moving on to pure malts* typical of a particular region, finishing with the most characteristic, to hone the tastebuds.

Any whisky lover will tell you the same thing: you are about to enter a world of great and varied richness, where the spectrum of tastes is infinite, and where the pleasure of discovering a new, untried whisky never fades.

Thierry Bénitah

ALPHABETICAL GUIDE

■ AGE
Every whisky has its age

What is the ideal age for a whisky? The answer to this question is a complex and subjective one. However one thing is certain: the way in which a whisky's age is defined. In the case of a non-vintage whisky it is the age of the youngest whisky in the blend. In fact all whiskies, with the exception of single cask* or single barrel whiskies are created from casks* of differing ages. Thus a twelve-year-old whisky may contain older whiskies: in whisky terms, twelve years and 364 days counts as twelve years.

For a vintage whisky, the age corresponds to the difference between the distillation date (the vintage) and the bottling date. Sometimes this is not mentioned on the label* and in these cases one has to trust in the honesty of the specialist seller. The vintage date is not a gauge of quality, as is the case with wine, but rather a piece of information which sometimes has symbolic value, for example as a special anniversary date. Whether it is a vintage or not, once bottled the whisky will not age any more; it can therefore either be laid down for later or drunk straight away.

The ideal age—if such a thing exists—is different for each type of whisky. A bourbon* or an Irish whiskey* rarely ages over fifteen years, whilst Scotch* and, in particular, certain pure malts*, can stand being aged for thirty years or more. The minimum legal age for Irish whiskeys and for Scotches is three years, for bourbons only two years. The optimum age for most Scotches is found somewhere between twelve and twenty years, whereas for bourbons and Irish whiskeys it is between four and twelve years. Nevertheless, one can find excellent eight-year-old Scotches and wonderful fifteen-year-old bourbons. Personal tastes are of great importance and the only essential thing is that everyone should be happy with their choice.

■ AGING
"The angel's share"

Everyone should have the chance at some point to step inside the cool air of a whisky storehouse and watch the light filtering down onto the rows of barrels. This twilight world forms part of the poetic side of whisky, as does the charming phrase "the angel's share," used to describe the evaporation of alcohol through the wood of the barrels. It is a poetic process but also a mysterious one, since the aging of the whisky is largely out of man's control. Nevertheless, we do know that the barrels and the climate play an essential role throughout this final stage in the whisky-making process. Only a few of the effects of climate have been discovered: the whisky will change more slowly in a humid climate than a dry one; significant variations in temperature accelerate the process of aging; and certain elements of the surrounding air also help the whisky to gain some of its defining features.

On the Isle of Islay* in Scotland*, iodine, salt, and sea-spray provide the perfect illustration of the environmental influence on aging. As the air seeps in through the pores in the wood, the alcohol undergoes a slow oxidization. This helps to set the future color*, aroma*, and flavor of the whisky. Although various laws set minimum aging periods, it is by regular tasting* from the casks that the best moment for bottling is decided. As evaporation diminishes the degree of alcohol slightly over the years, whisky often has spring water added to it to bring the Alcohol by Volume (ABV) to forty or forty-three percent.

Preceding pages:
Knockando
Distillery
in 1962.
Highlands,
Scotland.

Quality check
in the
storehouse of
the Royal
Lochnagar
Distillery.
Highlands,
Scotland.

■ Aroma

Discovering the aroma of a whisky is a very pleasurable moment. Usually the sensation in the nose precedes the flavor in the mouth, although not necessarily—these two impressions can sometimes be very different. While it is being made, whisky stores up aromas. First are the basic or primary aromas, inherent in the various grains* used (malt, corn, rye, etc.) Then come the secondary aromas, when the grain is changed into alcohol. The water, the different fuels used, the yeasts chosen for the fermentation*, and the type of distillation* all contribute to a large extent to the way in which the whisky acquires these fragrances. The tertiary aromas appear during aging in the barrel. The combination of all

three makes up the whisky's aromatic range. There are several main families of scent; as well as that contributed by the grain there are fruity (e.g. pear, raspberry, apricot); floral (e.g. violet, white flower, honeysuckle); woody (e.g. cedar, oak); vegetable (e.g. hay, heather, fresh grass); peaty (e.g. smoke, iodine, diesel fuel); mineral (e.g. gunflint, granite); spicy (e.g. pepper, cloves, ginger); and, finally, nutty aromas (e.g. walnut, hazelnut).

With a little experience, it is possible to judge the quality of a whisky simply by smelling it ("nosing"). This technique, used by the master blender* to select the malts* to be blended, involves the addition of a little water to the different whiskies being tested in order to release their aromas.

■ BLENDING
The art

Samuel Bronfman, founder of the Seagram commercial empire, used to say: "Distillation* is a science, but blending is an art." The blender is therefore an artist; he smells hundreds of samples and uses his impressive memory to create the best mixtures from them. Blending has a 170-year history, starting in 1831 with Aeneas Coffey's* invention of a still*, the "patent still," which was to allow the continuous production of grain alcohol*. Adopted by the Scottish, the blend, a mixture of grain* and malt* whiskies, has evolved and developed since 1840. Nowadays, more than ninety percent of the Scotches* drunk throughout the world are blends.

A blend is made up of between fifteen and forty different malts and two or three grain whiskies, the proportion of malt varying between twenty percent and forty percent of the mixture. The malts used in a blend belong to three categories: "base malts," which make up the heart of the blend; "flavoring malts" known by blenders for their strong personalities; and "packers," malts with subtle aromas*.

When a large proportion of old malts is included in the mixture, the term "luxury" is added to "blend." Blending takes place either after distillation or at the bottling stage, according to the choice of the distiller. The great branded blends, whose fame has continued to grow for over a century, include: Ballantine's, Bells, Chivas, Dewar's, Haig, Johnny Walker*, The Famous Grouse, and White Horse. Recently, dozens of blends of doubtful origin have appeared. Pale imitations of their glorious elders and betters, they are tarnishing the image of these superior whiskies.

Master distiller checking the quality of the alcohol, Jim Beam Distillery. Clermont, Kentucky, USA.

Advertisement for two blended brands: Dewar's, 1902, and John Haig, c. 1950.

■ Bootlegger

The origin of the term "boot-legger" stems from 1861, the time of the American Civil War, when unscrupulous indi-viduals sold illegally made bot-tles of alcohol to soldiers from the North and the South alike. It is said that these black-mar-keters hid the bottles of whisky in the legs of their boots. It was during the period of Prohibi-tion* between 1920 and 1933 that the bootleggers had their moment of glory, selling their wares through the "speakeasies" (secret bars where one had to speak quietly to avoid attracting attention), which had replaced regular bars. The speakeasies, of which there were many in New York—over 30,000 of them were counted—were not the only places where the contraband whisky flowed. Delicatessen workers, hairdressers, taxi drivers, and shoe-shine boys in the streets also acted as middlemen. The bootleggers generally imported their whisky from Scotland, Ireland, and Canada. The whisky-makers of these countries had escaped the Temperance Movement orchestrated by Lloyd George* and became, whether they admitted it or not, the allies of the bootleggers.

Alongside the importation by boat of Irish whiskeys* and Scotch*, some bootleggers of another kind, gangsters in the pay of Al Capone or Lucky Luciano, were having highly alcoholic hooch made in secret distilleries. The agents of the American Treasury Department, notably the infamous Eliot Ness, tried to destroy these by any means possible. The abolition of Prohibition in 1933 put paid to the illicit activities of the bootleggers.

Left: During Prohibition, even women's undergarments were used for smuggling alcohol.

Below: Police search a speakeasy, New York, 1926.

■ Bourbon

Strangely enough, Bourbon County in Kentucky*, which lends its name to the most famous American whiskey* in the world, has not had any distilleries for a long time. The county was created during the War of Independence (1775–1783) waged by the Americans against the English. It was in thanks for the help lent by French troops in the struggle that it was named bourbon, after the royal family then reigning in France. The first whiskeys produced in Kentucky were loaded into ships in Bourbon County and brought by boat to New Orleans. They arrived at their destination with the word "Bourbon" printed on each cask*; from then on, whiskey from Kentucky was known by this name.

Bourbon owes its fame to the Reverend Elijah Craig*. In 1789, he supposedly became the first person to distil a whisky from corn. Whether this is legend or reality, it is certainly true that the tradition has continued until the present day, since bourbon has to contain a minimum of fifty-one percent corn (see Grain). Its alcoholic strength after distillation* must not exceed eighty percent ABV and it must be aged for at least two years in new oak casks. To complete the regulations, it cannot be bottled if the alcoholic strength is below 40 percent. Most bourbons are straight whiskeys, which is to say that they are not cut with a neutral grain alcohol. Nowadays they are also all what is known as "sour mash"* whiskies.

The main bourbon-producing counties are found in Kentucky: Frankfort, Loretto, Bardstown, Clermont, Beam, Louisville, and Owensboro.

▉ Burns (Robert)

On January 25 every year, Scotland celebrates the anniversary of the birth of one of its greatest poets, Robert Burns. Born in 1759 in Alloway, not far from the town of Ayr, the capital of the Firth of Clyde in the Lowlands*, and at a time when it was considered unfashionable to have a Scottish accent and idioms, his poems and songs carried the flag for the Scottish language. His favorite themes were Scotland, women, friendship, religion, politics, the countryside, and, of course, whisky. His famous poem *John Barleycorn* is a veritable hymn to whisky. Burns stood up for the illicit distillers and throughout his life called for a reduction in the taxes* on whisky. "Freedom and whisky gangs together" was one of the favorite expressions of this poet, who was well loved by his compatriots. He conjures up images for us of smugglers distilling in secret and traveling up and down the Highland* trails to escape from the excisemen. This passionate man who loved life died on July 21, 1796 at Dumfries at the tender age of thirty-seven. Today, the Burns Heritage Trail, a tourist circuit that follows in the poet's footsteps, allows us to gaze at the landscape that inspired him.

▉ BUSHMILLS
The mother of all distilleries

Bushmills is claimed to be the oldest distillery in the world. Located in Country Antrim, not far from the Giants' Causeway (see map), it was the first in Ireland to gain an official license to make whiskey, on April 20, 1608. However Bushmills' success was a long time in coming. Bought by an independent merchant in 1860 for the modest sum of five hundred pounds, it was entirely destroyed by fire in 1885. It was not until 1923 when it was bought by Samuel Boyd, a wine and spirits merchant from Belfast, that its fortunes started to look up. Taken over in 1973 by the Irish Distillers group, Bushmills remains Northern Ireland's one and only distillery. However, this is by no means its only distinguishing feature; its buildings, topped by two pagoda-like towers (the kilns*), are in the purest Scottish style. As well as two highly regarded blends, Bushmills Original and Black Bush, Bushmills produces a ten-year-old single malt, a real rarity in Ireland. To the delight of the brand's enthusiasts, a Bushmills whiskey distilled in 1975 and christened "Millennium" was bottled in the year 2000.

Vintage advertisement for the Springbank Distillery in Campbeltown.

◼ Campbeltown

To the south of the Mull of Kintyre, the south-westerly Scottish peninsula, is Campbeltown, the place which gives its name to the whiskies of this wild, mountainous region (see map). Surprisingly enough, there are subtropical plants (including palm trees) in the area, whose presence is due to the climate—neither too hot in summer nor too cold in winter. Formerly a distiller's paradise, Campbeltown had over thirty distilleries at the end of the nineteenth century, thanks to its plentiful supply of barley, and of peat* and coal to use as fuel. However, overproduction, linked to a loss of interest in full-bodied malts*, variations in the quality of coal as well as its increasing scarcity, all contributed to the decline in Campbeltown malts to the point where nowadays only two distilleries survive: Glen Scotia and Springbank. Nevertheless, the regional classification remains. Springbank produces a second malt called Longrow, which is extremely peaty. Seldom bottled, this fine whisky resembles a malt from the Isle of Islay* and has a charm all of its own.

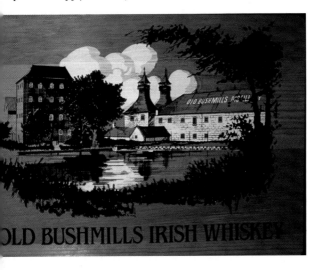

The Bushmills Distillery, Northern Ireland. Painting on wood.

■ CANADA

Ontario is the richest and most densely populated province in Canada and is the birthplace of Canadian whisky. It was in the town of Kingston (see map), between Toronto and Ottawa, that the first Canadian distilleries were created, in the mid-eighteenth century.

In 1858, the influential Hiram Walker* founded his first distillery next to Windsor, a town on the banks of Lake Erie, across the water from Detroit. This enthusiastic man brought style and identity to Canadian whiskies by launching the Canadian Club brand onto the market in 1884.

At the same time, the Seagram Company set up a distillery at Waterloo, also in Ontario. The company really took off in the 1930s, under the management of Samuel Bronfman. A genuine authority on whisky, he gave credibility to the process of blending*.

These days, the Seagram Company owns half a dozen distilleries in Canada. However the Hiram Walker Company has not been entirely outshone, having become the main shareholder in the Corby Distillery, known for its traditional Canadian whiskies. The other important Canadian whisky-producing companies are Alberta Distillers, Gilbey, Mc Guiness Distillers, Rieder, Brown Forman, and Schenley.

Canadian whiskies are, first and foremost, blends*. The best among them are made up in large part of rye* whiskies, of malted rye (dried, germinated rye), and a neutral alcohol. Often corn or malted barley-based whiskies are added. The distillation is carried out both in column stills* ("Coffey"* or "patent" stills) and in pot stills. The aging* takes place in oak casks* that have previously contained bourbon* or sherry. Canadian whiskies of inferior quality may be relatively weakly flavored, often tasting slightly of plum wine.

Canadian whiskies have a light, round, and fruity style tempered with a certain amount of bitterness. A classification system has been set up, which goes from A for top-of-the-range whiskies to E for those of inferior quality.

Seagram Company headquarters, Montreal.

■ CASKS
From new spirit to whisky

Originally, whiskies were not aged in casks, but drunk immediately after distillation*. It was by chance and thanks to the perceptiveness of certain producers that the casks, which had previously been used for transporting goods, were used for aging the new spirit, the newly produced alcohol. This practice only became universal towards the end of the nineteenth century.

The casks give color, roundness, and maturity to the whisky. The intensity of color*, aroma*, and flavor thus depend upon the age of the casks. As long as there is no law against it, a cask can be used up to three times. Bourbon* can only be aged in casks made of new oak, whose insides must be charred before being filled. Once emptied, the bourbon casks are not entirely useless; they are generally sent to distillers in Scotland* and Ireland* where they are used again for aging whisky. Casks that have contained fino, amontillado or oloroso sherry from the wine cellars of Andalusia are also used for this. For most whiskies, with the exception of bourbon, three types of cask are commonly used for aging: "barrels," casks that have previously contained bourbon and have

Cellars of the Royal Lochnagar Distillery. Highlands, Scotland.

a capacity of between 173 and 191 liters; "hogsheads," reconditioned casks with a capacity of 250 to 305 liters made of fresh oak or of wooden staves from barrels that have previously contained bourbon; and finally "sherry butts," with a 500-liter capacity that have contained sherry for at least four years. Around five percent of casks used are of this last type. Recently, producers have resorted to using casks that used to contain port, Madeira, rum, and even wine.

■ Cask strength

"Cask strength" means non-filtered, non-reduced whisky straight from the cask. In other words, a cask strength whisky has not been diluted with water at the distillery when bottled. This is why it can be up to sixty-three percent ABV (Alcohol by Volume, the alcohol content as a proportion of the total volume of liquid), whereas normally whisky is bottled at between forty percent and forty-three percent ABV. Cask strength whiskies are traditionally only available from independent bottlers, although some distillers are starting to put their own products directly onto the market. Many of these cask strength whiskies will actually come from one single cask*.

Though for some enthusiasts, cask strength whiskies bring together all that is best in whisky, others feel that the high alcohol content spoils the balance of the drink. A cask strength whisky may turn out to have a disagreeable smell, the aroma* having been destroyed by the quantity of alcohol. On the other hand if the right balance is maintained it makes an excellent liqueur*, to be drunk thoughtfully, and in moderation.

Cask strengths are more expensive than normal whiskies due to the rate of tax*, which is based on the percentage of alcohol, as well as the smaller number of bottles that each cask can fill. Finally, whisky has a tendency to go cloudy at low temperatures. This should not be a cause for concern, as it merely results from the fact that it has not been cold-filtered.

Whisky aged in a bourbon cask.

Clan

The word "clan" comes from the Gaelic "clann," meaning "child" or "lineage." Originally it was applied only to the family of a chief and those able to prove they shared common ancestry with him. Later on, the clan was extended to include those who recognized a chief's authority and placed themselves under his protection. The history of the clan is closely linked to that of Scotland* and, in particular, the Highlands*.

The first clans date back to the eleventh century. Originally an administrative system, separation into clans allowed a census to be made of the population. With time, differences grew between the clans and rivalries were born. The less powerful clans allied themselves to the dominant clans who, conversely, sometimes subdivided themselves. Thus the famous clan of the MacDonalds who proclaimed themselves Lords of the Islands gave birth to the MacDonalds of Clanranald and Glencoe.

Their distinguishing badge was tartan, a woolen material patterned in large colored squares. Over a thousand varieties have been counted, each of which represents a certain clan. In 1579 the Scottish parliament voted in a law limiting the right to distil to the noble families of the country. It was thus to the clans that this privilege fell. In 1707, following Scotland's enforced incorporation into Britain, the majority of the Highland clans rebelled. Among other reprisals, the government introduced a law forbidding the clans to wear tartan or kilts, the traditional Highland clothing. This dark period in Scottish history ended with the repeal of the law in 1782.

At the start of modern era the clans started to make peace. Nowadays, far from having fallen into disuse, they have enjoyed a renaissance, spurred on in part by Scottish independence movements. Every major event in Scotland is now a reason to show one's membership of a clan by wearing all the traditional regalia of kilts and tartan.

Club

The consumer society, the development of superstores, and extensive media coverage, have all combined to make certain so-called "luxury" products everyday and commonplace. This process has, however, aroused the curiosity of the consumer, and whisky (Scottish malts* in particular) has become a particular focus of interest. In response to the growing demand for information and training, clubs were created at the beginning of the 1980s to bring together beginners and connoisseurs. More and more special-interest clubs are opening whose main focus is on the pleasure of sharing a tasting* session with

Cecil Aldin, *The Hunt Dinner*, England, early twentieth century. Private collection.

friends. All operating more or less on the same model, they bring their members together around one, or often, several whiskies specially selected for their individual characters, whose merits and demerits are then passionately discussed.

Certain clubs, such as the Scotch Malt Whisky Society, based in Edinburgh, favor a certain style of whisky. Others are more general. Most aim to make a profit, except for certain corporate clubs such as the highly prestigious Keepers of the Quaich (Beaconsfield). This club brings together Scotch whisky professionals from around the world at enormous banquets in Scotland. Similar clubs exist in the United States*: the Kentucky Bourbon Circle (Clermont) is, as its name suggests, a meeting-place for lovers of bourbon*.

A distillery, c. 1900. Lithograph. Bibliothèque des Arts décoratifs, Paris.

COFFEY (AENEAS)
The patent still revolution

In 1831, Aeneas Coffey, an Irishman of French descent, created a still* which allowed the continuous distillation* of grain alcohol*. This retired customs official had perfected the "patent still," a patent filed several years earlier by Robert Stein, a famous Lowlands* distiller. His invention was to revolutionize the whisky industry.

Coffey first offered it to the Irish, who rejected it, feeling that whiskies produced by the patent still lacked character. However, the Scottish—and notably Andrew Usher*, the man who was to popularize blends*—saw in this new process the chance to produce less distinctive alcoholic beverages than malts* in great quantity and at low prices, which would allow

them to conquer the English and foreign markets. The results exceeded even their wildest expectations. The "patent still," in contributing to the success of Scottish blends, assured the supremacy of Scotch* over its Irish rival.

The Canny
Man pub,
Edinburgh.

Collecting

Whisky is a collector's item in the same way as are stamps, coins, or matchboxes. The whisky collector is not the inveterate drinker one might imagine; he or she is endowed with a keen sense of detail. A simple change in the name of the importer or the color of the label* is enough to set him or her off on the hunt for new acquisitions.

Packaging* is important and everything associated with it provides an excuse for adding to the collection: bottles, of course, but also labels, metal boxes, glasses with brand* names on them, miniature bottles, and so on.

The miniature bottle collector is certainly the most common.

Collecting reduced-sized bottles takes up less space, and generally is not too expensive. However, some miniature bottles can cost several hundred dollars!

Of course, different brands have their own importance and are not all of equal worth in the eyes of the collector. Thus, for example, among Tennessee* whiskeys, Jack Daniel's* is particularly sought after, as is Macallan among malts. Certain old Macallan bottles fetch over $7,000 at auction. Collectors from the four corners of the globe meet up and get to know one another; they even form collectors' clubs*. One of them, the Mini Bottle Club, unites collectors of miniature whisky and other spirits bottles from around the world.

WEIGHTS AND MEASURES ACT 1985
Unless Supplied Pre-Packed
GIN RUM VODKA WHISKY
Are offered for sale or served in these premises
in quantities of
ONE-QUARTER OF A GILL
OR MULTIPLES THEREOF

■ Color

Whisky offers an impressive range of colors, ranging from almost clear to purplish amber, with all the shades of yellow, gold, and amber in between. Since the alcohol leaving the still is colorless, it is during the aging process that the future whisky takes on its color. The type of cask* used is the most important factor. The aging of bourbons* in new oak casks rapidly brings about the color of the whisky which, from the age of two years onwards, is lightly amber in tone.

New spirit, still colorless, leaving the still.

The use of sherry casks allows a range of colors to be obtained. A cask of sherry fino will produce gold with hints of amber, while at the other extreme a cask of sherry oloroso will yield a dark amber color. Pre-used casks produce light whiskies whose intensity rarely goes beyond strong yellows; casks that have contained port can give the whisky a pink tinge. The addition of caramel is a legal practice used fairly often for coloring everyday blends*. This practice has only a slight influence on the taste* and gives the whisky an artificial amber color.

The transparent glass used for most bottles allows one to admire the different shades of color. Certain amber whiskies evoke a symphony of autumnal colors, with subtle shades of yellow, green, and brown. The vocabulary used to define a whisky's colors is infinite: white wine, straw yellow, vivid yellow, light gold, vivid gold, gold with green tones, medium amber, dark amber, golden brown, reddish brown, and so on.

Tom Wesselmann, *Still Life I*, 1962. Nierendorf Gallery, Berlin.

■ Combination

Whisky can be combined with various foods and other products. Some combinations are tried and tested, others may appear more exotic. Among those that are well known, one of the most widely appreciated is that of whisky and smoked fish. The whole skill lies in the choice of whisky. Thus with a Scottish salmon, a lightly smoked whisky from the Isle of Islay* such as Bunnahabhain or Bruichladdich would be the perfect match. The obvious mixture of whisky and haggis, the famous Scottish dish made of stuffed sheep's belly, is also a real delicacy. The ill-informed will tell you that whisky tones down the strong taste of haggis. On the contrary it actually brings out the flavor, which can be complemented still further with a puree of potatoes and turnip. Whisky can be used for cooking meats, and cooked cheese has an interesting and surprising affinity with sherry-cask whisky. Another remarkable combination is that of chocolate and whisky, which is one of the rare alcoholic drinks able to hold its own with the smell and taste of the cocoa bean. With a praline ganache, opt for an old single malt*, for example a sherry-cask whisky with notes of nuts and dry fruit. Lastly, the most famous of cocktails, Irish Coffee—a marriage between coffee and whisky—is in a sense the ultimate combination. For preference choose an arabica coffee and a Paddy or John Power's* Irish whiskey. Don't forget to add brown sugar and whipped cream. At the end of a meal, a cigar and a well-chosen whisky go together wonderfully.

Consumption

Blended* Scotch* has the highest consumption of whisky in the world, with almost a billion bottles sold in 1995. The United States and the United Kingdom share top place as the most fervent whisky drinkers, ahead of Spain, France* and Japan*. After Scotch comes American whiskey; almost fifty percent of the 400 million

Drinking whisky in a 1940s bar in America.

bottles sold in 1995 went to the United States*, whose consumption is far ahead of Japan, Germany, and Australia. Canadian whisky takes third place with 300 million bottles sold in 1995, of which 225 million went to the United States and only 45 million to Canada*. Single malts* and Irish whiskeys are neck and neck with almost forty million bottles sold each in 1995.

France, surprisingly, is the greatest consumer of malts* in the world, ahead of the United Kingdom and Italy.

The Republic of Ireland* consumes twenty percent of the whiskey it produces, the United Kingdom, the States, and France absorbing a further thirty percent between them.

Other producing countries such as Japan, India, Brazil, and Thailand consume almost all they produce. Whether genuine whiskies or not, between them they sold 500 million bottles in 1995.

During the same period, the consumption of American whiskeys has stagnated whilst Canadian whisky sales have fallen by twenty percent.

■ Craig (Elijah)

History shows that religion and whisky have sometimes gone hand in hand. In Ireland*, Saint Patrick* supposedly introduced the art of distillation in the fifth century. In Scotland*, Pastor Magnus Eunson* was the most famous smuggler of the eighteenth century, and many historians claim that the American Baptist pastor Elijah Craig was the creator of bourbon*.

Born in Virginia, Elijah Craig (1743–1808) settled in Kentucky* in 1786. Three years later, he started distilling a whiskey* made from corn, inspired by Nohelick, an alcoholic drink made by Indians. He was also the first to use a mixture of corn, barley, and rye as well as charred oak casks to make his whiskey.

Craig went on to create a distillery in Georgetown and the bourbon he produced there was considered the best in the United States*. In 1795, a fine of $140 was imposed on him for producing whiskey without a license. After this episode, nothing further was heard from Elijah Craig until his death in 1808.

At the end of the nineteenth century the American whiskey producers liked to recall the story of this pioneer. What better moral figurehead than a religious distiller to silence the protests of the prohibitionists? In order to immortalize this symbolic character, the Heaven Hill Distillery named one of its whiskies Elijah Craig.

■ Daniel (Jack)

Jack Daniel (1846–1909), abandoned by his parents at the age of five, was brought up in Lincoln County by a couple of farmer distillers, Dan and Mary Jane Call. It was there that "Little Jack" (a nickname he owed to his diminutive stature) learnt the art of distillation* from a slave by the name of Nearest Green.

Around 1860, Dan Call handed his distillery over to Jack, who bought some land near Lynchburg, in Lincoln County, and officially founded the Jack Daniel Distillery in 1866. People say that Alfred Eaton perfected a filtering process unique to Tennessee* whiskies when the distillery was set up, for Jack Daniel's is not a bourbon* but a Tennessee* whiskey. Helped by his nephew, Lem Motlow, Daniel developed the market for his whiskey, which in 1904 won a gold medal in a show in Louisiana. Subsequently, the brand became international and continued to win prizes. When Jack Daniel died in 1909, his cousin Dick Daniel and Lem Motlow took up the torch. In 1910, Tennessee was proclaimed a "dry"

state (it was forbidden to produce whiskey but not to drink it), which led to the closure of the distillery until 1938. Although Jack Daniel was bought by the spirits* group Brown-Forman, the Motlow family continued to run the distillery.

There are two versions of this whiskey: Green Label*, which is not available in Europe, and Black Label. Both have always proudly sported the number 7, although the origin of this tradition is a mystery. Some say it is in tribute to a friend who had seven shops, others think it is in memory of seven casks that were lost and finally found again. This enigma contributes

to the Jack Daniel myth, which charms collectors throughout the world.

■ DCL

The creation, on April 24, 1877, of the Distillers Company Limited (DCL) marks a decisive turning point in the history of Scottish whisky. This society, made up of merchants and distillers, brought together the Haig, Dewar's, Buchanan, Johnnie Walker*, and White Horse companies for the first time. Its guiding principle was the production of quality whiskies.

Spurred on by its young CEO, William H. Ross, DCL bought up trading companies and distilleries that were experiencing difficulties because of the successive whisky industry crises in the first half of the twentieth century: Prohibition*, the rise in taxes*, and the two World Wars. By 1927 DCL had become the owner of the main blended* brands and of a third of Scottish distilleries. After the Second World War DCL's dominance was confirmed. Four of its brands, Johnnie Walker, Dewar's, Cutty Sark, and J&B represented almost half of the world sales of Scotch* at the beginning of the 1960s.

Towards 1980, recession hit DCL hard, with the result that in 1986 it was taken over by the Guinness group. This group attempted to revive sales at DCL, which became United Distillers. In 1988 the launch of a range of six single* malts christened the "Classic Malts" achieved considerable success. Strengthened by this victory, the United Distillers group continued to make innovations at the same time as conquering

DISTILLATION

new markets with its blended* brands, which remain an inexhaustible source of profits.

■ Distillation

Distillation, the fourth stage in the manufacture of whisky, consists in transforming the ground and fermented grains into a high proof alcohol. Two types of still* are used: the "pot still" for non-continuous distillation, and the patent, or Coffey*, still for continuous distillation. For pure malts* (malted barley), distillation is carried out in the pot stills. The "wash" is sent to the first still, the "wash still." It is heated directly by a naked flame or by steam until it evaporates. As they heat up, the alcohol vapors separate from the wash. When condensed, they produce a distillate, called "low wines," which are twenty-eight percent ABV. The second phase of distillation then begins: the low wines pass into a glass-fronted box, the "spirit safe," which allows the distiller to control the purity of the alcohol and to remove the first distilled spirits (the "foreshots") as well as the

last (the "feints"). Only the main body of the distillation (the "middle cut") is moved on to the second still, the "spirit still." The foreshots and the feints are redistilled with the next batch of low wines. The alcohol coming from the spirit still is, on average, sixty-eight percent ABV, and will be brought to around 63.5 percent ABV by the addition of water* from the distillery before being put into casks* to age.

Some distilleries use triple distillation. For example, to make Springbank, the famous single* malt from Campbeltown*, the foreshots and feints are distilled in a third still and the alcohol thus obtained is incorporated with that from the second still. The patent still continues producing for as long as it is supplied with fermented grain* and steam, and allows very high-yield distillation. Single grain* alcohols, like American whiskeys, are distilled with the patent, or Coffey, still. For the distillation of certain of its whiskies, the Midleton* distillery in Ireland* combines the pot still and the patent still.

Jack Daniel Distillery warehouse. Tennessee, USA.

Monitoring alcohol purity in the spirit safe.

Eunson (Magnus)

Following the example of French monks who were vineyard owners and excellent winemakers, some Scottish pastors contributed greatly to whisky's success. Towards the end of the eighteenth century, Magnus Eunson, one of the most famous among them, was distilling in secret in the Orkneys in the little town of Kirkwall, in the same place where several years later the Highland Park Distillery was to be created.

This character embodied the freedom-hungry temperament of the Scottish people to such an extent that his name was known throughout the country. It seems that Magnus Eunson always knew how to trick the tax agents, using the most incredible ploys to outwit them: people say that one day he escaped justice at the hands of the law by carrying out a funeral service in front of a casket full of whisky bottles! History does not tell whether whisky helped give him inspiration for his sermons, but it was said that there was always a bottle of it in his pulpit.

Fermentation

Fermentation is the third stage of the whisky-making process and takes place by transforming sugar into alcohol.

The "grist" mixed with hot water creates a "mash," which becomes a "wort" after mashing; the wort is then put into enormous vats called "wash backs." These vats, traditionally made from Oregon pine, are nowadays often made of stainless steel. Easier to maintain, they also allow greater control of fermentation. Some distilleries, however, remain faithful to wooden vats; others, after having tried stainless steel, go back to wood because of its better thermal exchange. Yeast is then added to the wort. The selected yeast is of the *Saccharomyces Cerevisiae* type, which allows fermentation to begin more rapidly and makes sure that it continues as it should. After the yeast starts working, fermentation soon becomes frenzied. Stirring rods continuously mix up the wort to stop the temperature from getting too high: under no

Fermentation of the wort. Jack Daniel Distillery, Tennessee, USA.

development that this entails. At the end of fermentation, which lasts between forty-seven and forty-eight hours, the sugar is transformed into alcohol. The fermented wort (the

circumstances must it go above 95 to 98°F (35° to 37°C) as the yeast would then be inhibited and fermentation would stop, with all the risks of bacterial

Fermentation of the wort. Lagavulin Distillery, Isle of Islay.

"wash") is then at eight percent proof and is no more nor less than a malt beer. After this the wash is put in "wash charger" vats before distillation*.

Royal
Lochnagar
whisky.

■ Glasses

Wine enthusiasts will tell you that there is nothing like a Burgundy or Bordeaux glass to bring out the best in a great wine. The same goes for whiskies, especially the Scottish malts*. Up to a few years ago, the only glass used was a straight, rather heavy one, with a thick bottom and a flat base, known as a "tumbler." This is still the most widely used nowadays; it is ideal for blended* Scotch*, because water or ice can be added to it. In pubs, the "dram," a little glass with a thick bottom and a cylindrical shape is the most commonly used. This is the "saloon" style whisky glass, made famous by 1950s Westerns (see Literature and Cinema).

These two types of glass, quite aside from all aesthetic considerations, do not really do justice to whisky. The aroma of Scottish malts* and certain bourbons* is enhanced when they are tasted from slightly tapered narrow glasses. Distillers and master blenders, who understand this, use a sherry glass called a copita. Similar to the Bordeaux glass but less bulky, it has a fairly short stem and a characteristic tulip form. An "Inao" enological glass is equally well adapted. The list would not be complete without the "Quaich." Of Celtic origin, it is in some ways the Scottish equivalent of the wine-tasting cup, except that it has two handles. Traditionally made of silver, it can also be found in pewter. The Scots use it at the ceremonial celebration of haggis, the famous dish of stuffed sheep's belly. According to tradition, after having read a text by Robert Burns*, with glass of whisky in hand, the company drinks a toast to the poet's memory, crying "Slàinte!" (Cheers!)

"Inspiring bold John Barleycorn!
What dangers thou canst make us scorn!
Wi' tippenny, we fear nae evil;
Wi' usquebae, we'll face the devil!"

Robert Burns, *Tam O'Shanter*

■ Glenlivet

Even before the creation of a legal distillery, the reputation of Glenlivet (the valley of the Livet, the famous river running through Speyside in Scotland), was already made. At the beginning of the eighteenth

century more than two hundred stills were producing illicit whisky there.

The excisemen had great difficulty in convincing the illicit distillers of the immorality of their acts, since everyone knew that the King, George IV, was a great lover of illicit whisky. Urged on by the Duke of Gordon, the area's landowner, the government voted in the Excise Act of 1823 to legalize distillation*. Once this law had been adopted, the Duke encouraged George Smith, one of his tenant farmers, to set up a legal distillery at Upper Drumin, which took the name of Glenlivet. It was reconstructed in 1858 at Minmore, in the heart of the Livet valley. Independent until 1935, Glenlivet was taken over by the Canadian Seagram group in 1978.

Many distilleries used the name Glenlivet, so to avoid potential confusion a decree of 1880 gave the sole right to use this name to the Minmore Distillery. However, the other distilleries were allowed to use Glenlivet as a suffix to their names.

Glenlivet whisky is as fine and delicate as the two other whiskies of the valley: Braes of Glenlivet and Tamnavulin.

George Smith, anonymous.

Duke George Gordon, George Sanders. Goodwood collection, Goodwood, England.

Traction engines transporting Glenlivet whisky, c. 1920.

■ GRAIN
The raw material of whisky

The raw material common to all whiskies is grain. Whiskies are made from only one type of grain in the case of pure malts* and from a mixture of grains in the case of bourbons*, Irish whiskeys*, blended Scottish* whiskies, and Canadian whiskies*.

In Ireland* up until the beginning of the twentieth century, five types of grain were used: barley, malted barley, oats, corn, and rye. The small proportion of malted barley used in making Irish whiskeys meant that mashing took a long time. Nowadays, corn and rye are hardly used except for making bourbons.

Though almost all grains are used to some extent, there is one among them, barley, which remains indispensable, and is found in all whiskies. Barley is rich in starch, an essential element in the mashing and fermentation processes; the most important grain for Scottish whisky, it was originally grown on land belonging to the distilleries. The last few years have seen the appearance of many new varieties of barley, which are both cheaper and easier to harvest. The Macallan Distillery refuses to use them, remaining faithful to the traditional varieties. However, it is something of an exception as it is not unusual for distillers to make their whiskies from imported grains. Purists object strongly to this, on the grounds that the grain is to whisky what the grape is to wine! This, however, is perhaps something of an exaggeration.

Nevertheless, the grain used plays a role in deciding the aroma* and taste* of the whisky: corn (maize), the base of bourbon, brings sweetness to whiskey; rye brings bitterness to Canadian ryes*; barley, more complex, brings dryness or sweetness depending on whether or not peat* is used in the malting* process.

Preceding double page: ears of barley.

Isle of Skye, Highlands, Scotland.

■ Grain (single)

The least well-known Scottish whiskies are the single grains. This is largely because they are rarely bottled on their own, usually being employed solely for making blends*. Single grains come from only one distillery. They are made up of eighty-five percent corn and non-malted barley to which rye and wheat are sometimes added. These grains are ground into a thick flour and cooked in order to release their starch (see Malting). Once the cooking is finished, they are put into a water* mixture which also contains 15 percent malted barley or green malt (undried malted barley), as decided by the distiller. After mashing* and fermentation*, distillation* is carried out in the patent stills. The alcohol obtained is a maximum of 94.8 percent ABV, and though very pure has a fairly neutral taste*. Aging* allows it to fulfill its potential in terms of taste and aroma. Single grains are distinguished by their lightness and delicacy. They can serve as the ideal introduction to Scotch whiskies*. The main distilleries that offer single grain whiskies are Invergordon, North British, Girvan, and Cameron Bridge.

■ Highlands

The Highlands (see map) are the largest region in Scotland*, in terms of surface area and also, if one includes Speyside*, in terms of number of distilleries. In the extreme north, the rugged Shetland Islands, a paradise for birds, provide a sharp contrast to the lakes and the fertile land of the counties of Perth in the south, and Aberdeen in

the east. In the center, the Grampians mountain range rivals Ben Nevis in the west, the highest summit in the United Kingdom at 4400 feet (1,344 m). On a clear day, the view stretches to the Isles of the West—Skye, Jura, and Mull.

The Highland whiskies are all made north of a line running between Greenock in the west, and Dundee in the east. The Midlands, situated to the north of this line, produce light malts*, floral with a trace of peat*. The well-known distilleries of the Midlands are Glenturret, which produces a tasty pure malt with almond aromas*, Edradour, the smallest distillery in Scotland, Aberfeldy, Blair Atholl, and Tullibardine. To the east are balanced malts like the Royal Lochnagar, situated near Balmoral, the summer residence of the Queen. The North Highlands take us from Inverness near Loch Ness to the Orkneys. It is there that the delicious Highland Park, with its aromas of peat and heather, and Scapa, a lighter, more chocolaty malt, are made. Back on the mainland is Old Pulteney, characterized by its aging in manzanilla sherry casks*, Clynelish which can be very peaty, Balblair and the very famous distillery of Glenmorangie with its extremely elegant malt that the Scots adore. Finally, the West Highlands are known above all for their island whiskies: Talisker on the Isle of Skye, a prestigious malt with notes of spices, and of the seas; Isle of Jura, a lighter whisky; and Ledaig, a fine, exquisite malt from the Isle of Mull.

Independent bottler

As well as the "official" whiskies of the distilleries there are also whiskies bottled on behalf of individual merchants. Whiskies bottled for distilleries have higher world sales figures but the merchants, known as "independent bottlers," still survive, buying whisky in cask* from distilleries and bottling it themselves.

For a long time they were the only ones who offered single malts*, until the day the producers realized the potential of the market. Despite this new competition, independent bottlers continue to offer a very wide choice of malts*. Due to their flexibility they can regularly offer new variations and limited series, which are particularly appreciated by enthusiasts and collectors. Some independent bottlers have acquired international fame. This is the case with Gordon & Macphail, whose specialty is buying whiskies in cask* and then aging them in its own cellars. This company also possesses a unique stock of whisky casks containing old whiskies. Cadenhead and Signatory Vintage are two of the most dominant companies, though there are also dozens of smaller-scale merchants. An independent bottler is recognizable by the elegantly presented label that is fixed to its bottles, on which only the name of the distillery varies.

For several years, independent bottlers have been finding it difficult to buy casks. What is more, some producers forbid them to use the name of the distilleries, choosing to forget their major role in the current success of malts.

Hopefully an agreement will be reached, so that the public will be able to benefit for a long time yet from their experience and their entrepreneurial spirit.

Harry's bar, Paris.

Irish whiskey is the oldest in the world! This claim always has been, and always will be a point of contention between the Irish and the Scots.

Whatever the truth may be, every March 17, the Irish throw themselves into celebrating St. Patrick's* Day. Legend has it that this monk introduced the art of distillation* into Ireland in 432 A.D.

The English invasion of 1170 allowed Irish whiskey to break free of its national borders, and by the end of the seventeenth century the country had two thousand distilleries, mainly illicit. It was during this truly golden age that the Jameson* and John Power* distilleries were created.

However, from 1832 onwards, Irish whiskey started to show signs of decline, to the benefit of Scottish blends*. Two events helped accelerate this decline: the Civil War in 1916 closed the doors of the British market and Prohibition* in the United States* (1920–1933) interrupted Irish whiskey exports to its main market. In order to reverse the decline, the Cork Distilleries Company merged in 1973 with the Irish Distillers group, which had just taken over the Bushmills Distillery. In 1988 the Pernod Ricard group acquired Irish Distillers. Today there

are three centers of distillation in Ireland: Midleton* in the south near Cork, Cooley in the center, not far from Dundalk, and Bushmills*, the first official distillery, in Ulster.

Irish whiskeys are practically all blends* but in contrast to blended Scotch, the mixture is made up of barley and malt*. Oats, rye, and corn are hardly used at all any more. The proportions vary according to the brand.

The other difference between brands is the type of distillation used. At Bushmills, the wash is distilled three times in medium-sized pot stills*. At Cooley it is distilled twice, as in Scotland*, which gives a less powerful alcohol. At Midleton, as well as the classic triple distillation, certain whiskeys can be distilled up to five times, going through both the pot still and patent still.

To gain the right to the title "Irish whiskey," the alcohol has to age for a minimum of three years in the cask. Irish whiskey is generally aged in sherry casks or casks which have contained bourbon*. The Irish have carefully studied the quality of aging* and have brought their stock of casks up to date. They have even considered the idea of declaring a vintage for their most prestigious whiskeys.

Above left: A bottle of Jameson's twelve-year-old whiskey.
Right: Connemara, c. 1890.

Portnahaven,
Isle of Islay,
south-west
of Scotland.

Islay

This name is the subject of a real cult among lovers of single malts*, and it is on this island that the peatiest whiskies in the world are produced. Islay, 25 miles long, lies off the south-west coast of Scotland*. Extensively covered in the precious peat* used for drying the malt, it has had up to eight distilleries in the past, five of which are still in use.

The water* from the springs which supply the distilleries runs through the peat fields, absorbing the scent of peat; it is also enriched by the sea—iodine, sea spray, and salt permeate the soil. Here more than anywhere else, the role of the geological and climatic elements is fundamental. To pour oneself a pure malt from the Isle of Islay is to capture in the glass* the power of the ocean... The names of the distilleries are highly evocative—Laphroaig, Lagavulin, Bruichladdich, Bunnahabhain, Caol Ila, Bowmore, and Ardbeg.

The Port Ellen Distillery stopped all production in 1983, but its malting floors continued to be used by the other distilleries on the island. As for Ardbeg and Bruichladdich, they closed down for a while but happily both have reopened in the last few years.

Jameson (John)

Historians still argue these days about the exact origin of the Jameson* Distillery: John Jameson may not be the founder. It is thought that this young man of Scottish origin landed in the Dublin region in around 1770. Ten years later he

bought the Bow Street Distillery from a certain John Stein and founded the John Jameson and Son Company. His two sons John and William took over from him, William managing the neighboring Marrowbone Lane Distillery. The Jamesons transformed the family company into a veritable empire and the distillery continued to grow throughout the nineteenth century.

The whiskey* produced at this time, considered as one of the best in Ireland, was distilled twice in enormous pot stills*, capable of producing 4.5 million liters of whiskey a year. However, it was not until 1963 that a whiskey appeared on the market bearing the name of the distillery, the Crested Ten by John Jameson and Son. In fact all production up until that point had been destined for independent bottlers* who marketed their whiskeys themselves.

The Jameson brand was launched in 1968, two years after the merger with the Power's* and Cork Distilleries* companies. Three years later, Bow Street closed its doors for the last time and the Power's Distillery became responsible for the production of the famous Jameson's, which was finally transferred to Midleton* after Power's had also shut down. In the middle of the 1980s, in memory of a wonderful twelve-year-old whiskey produced in Bow Street, the Jameson 1780, was on the market. Characterized by sherry and spices, this whiskey resembled its glorious ancestor produced at Bow Street.

Casks being rolled towards the storehouses of the Jameson Distillery. Dublin, 1971.

■ JAPAN

In seventy-five years Japan has become one of the greatest whisky-producing and whisky-drinking nations on the planet. Two men are responsible for the development of Japanese whisky, Masataka Taketsuru, born in 1894, and Shinjiro Torii, born in 1878, founder of the Suntory company.

Whilst studying chemistry at Glasgow University, Taketsuru gained such a passion for whisky that he learnt the art of distillation. Married to a Scottish woman, he returned to Japan in 1921 and was hired by Shinjiro Torii, a major winegrower. In 1923, with Taketsuru's help, this man founded the first Japanese distillery in the Yamazaki valley, near Kyoto. In 1934, Taketsuru created his own company, Nikka, and set up his first distillery on the northern island of Hokkaido.

It was at the beginning of the 1950s that Japanese whisky really took off. Currently, four major groups share the market: Suntory, Nikka, Sunraku Ocean, and Kirin Seagram, the newest arrival.

Japanese whiskies follow to a large extent in the Scottish tradition. The manufacturing techniques of the two countries are very similar and Japanese distilleries import Scottish malts* destined for the mixture of their own blends*. But, more and more, their whiskies have acquired their own personality, thanks notably to the quality and exceptional purity of their spring waters*, the presence of peat* in Hokkaido, a cutting edge technology, and a very high level of human expertise. Japanese whiskies are distinguished by their clear, malty taste, a subtle smokiness, and a degree of roundness and sweetness in the mouth. The Japanese drink their whisky with plenty of added water.

Just as enterprising abroad as at home, the Japanese have bought up Scottish distilleries, including Bomore on the Isle of Islay*, and Tomatin in the north of the Highlands*, the biggest distillery in Scotland. But it is in Japan itself that the world's largest distillery is to be found: Suntory Hakushu, whose distillation* room contains twenty-four stills*.

Above: A bottle of twelve-year-old Suntory Yamazaki, the most famous of Japanese whiskies. Right: Nikka Distillery at Yoichi, Hokkaido Island.

■ Kentucky

Kentucky is the land of bourbon*, the most famous of all American whiskeys*. Contrary to popular belief, bourbons do not necessarily have to be made in Kentucky, even though these days they all are.

In 1769, the famous explorer Daniel Boon undertook the settlement of Kentucky, which was at that stage uninhabited. This region officially became the fifteenth State of the Union in 1792. It was a land of welcome for the whiskey producers of Pennsylvania, North Carolina, and Virginia, where the first whiskeys were made. They came to Kentucky fleeing taxes levied by George Washington to pay off the debts of the new nation.

Kentucky, sometimes called the "granite region," was perfectly suited to the development of a whiskey industry. Its soil, rich in phosphates, is suitable for growing grain*: maize, wheat, or rye*. The river water*, rich in calcium, is extremely pure. As for the climate, very hot in summer and cold in winter, it is very conducive to aging* in casks*. Finally, the region is covered in forests full of the oak trees used for making casks.

Before Prohibition*, there were several hundred distilleries in Kentucky. Today, only nine active ones remain: Ancient Age, Barton, Jim Beam, Bernheim, Early Times, Four Roses, Heaven Hill, Maker's Mark, and Wild Turkey. They are situated very close together, bordered in the east by Frankfort, the state capital, and in the west by Bardstown and Louisville.

■ Kiln

If when coming round the corner of a path you see a form in the distance that reminds you of a pagoda, don't be surprised—you're still in Scotland! Mounted on distilleries, these towers, or kilns, are used for malting*.

The bottom part of the kiln is an open oven which allows the smoke of the peat* fire to permeate the malt during drying (in Ireland*, where peat is not used, the oven is closed). Above the oven are floors traditionally made of perforated tiles designed to let the smoke pass through slowly. At the top, the roof of the kiln is equipped with fans to expel the smoke. The absence of any fans on the kiln roofs of the

Ardbeg Distillery has much to do with the very peaty flavor of this malt. These days, few distilleries malt their own barley and the kilns are used less and less. Some have even been classified as historic monuments, others have been transformed into stylish residences like at Saint Magdalene, a former distillery in the Scottish Lowlands*.

Above: View of the kilns of the Port Ellen Distillery, Isle of Islay, Scotland.

Left: The Jim Beam Distillery. Frankfort, Kentucky, USA.

"Is it to be the last?" he said.
"O, yes, positively," said Little Chandler.
"Very well, then," said Ignatius Gallaher, *"let us have another one as a* **deoc an dorius**—*that's good vernacular for a small whisky, I believe."*

James Joyce, *Dubliners*

■ Label

The label is a whisky bottle's identity card. On it are found the normal mentions of origin (Scotch, Irish, American, Canadian), the type of whisky (bourbon*, blend*, malt*, rye*, etc.) and the age* (with or without vintage). Certain more specific pieces of information need to be explained. To have the right to be called Scotch or bourbon, the alcohol content as a proportion of the total volume of liquid must not be less than forty percent. Conversely, whisky rarely has an alcohol content higher than sixty-three percent. Certain whiskies carry the word "proof" (alcoholic content). In the United States a whiskey that is 100 percent proof corresponds to a fifty percent alcohol by volume level. Under the old, more complex British system, 100 percent proof equals fifty-seven percent alcohol by volume.

Certain high-proof whiskies carry the word "cask strength"*, which proves that they have not been diluted with the distillery's water*. They sometimes come from a single cask, in which case the title "single cask"* or "single barrel" is mentioned on the label along with the number of the cask and bottle. The volume must also be stated. In Europe seventy centiliters is the current norm; in the United States, seventy-five centiliters is more usual. Finally, the phrases "bottled in," "distilled and bottled in," and "genuine" provide the assurance that the whisky was distilled and bottled in its country of origin. Rather pompous comments such as

Label for a Scottish whisky, c. 1880. Bibliothèque des Arts décoratifs, Paris.

Illicit distillery, USA, c. 1920.

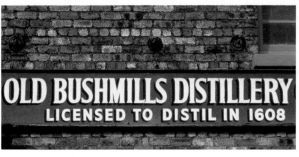

"superior," "very old," or "original" have no meaning other than that which the producer or the independent bottler* chooses to give them. The comment "sour mash"* is superfluous since, nowadays, all whiskies are sour mash.

License

Taxed* from very early on, whisky distillation* fluctuated between legality and illegality for a long time. Up until the end of the eighteenth century, illicit distillation was more prevalent, as much in Ireland* as in Scotland*.

Ireland can pride itself on possessing the oldest distillery in the world since, on April 20, 1608, Sir Thomas Philipps, owner of the Bushmills* Distillery, obtained a license giving him the right to distill *uisge beatha** for a period of seven years. However, it was not until the creation of the Jameson* Distillery in 1780 and John Power's* Distillery in 1791 that "official whiskey" overthrew poteen*, an illicitly distilled alcohol.

In Scotland the first license was granted by the parliament in 1690 to a certain Duncan Forbes of Culloden. Nevertheless, illicit distillation continued to develop and in 1780 in Edinburgh alone there were over four hundred illicit stills*. The Wash Act of 1784, and the Excise Act of 1823, with its reduction of taxes, encouraged the illicit stills to become legal. In 1824, George Smith, founder

of Glenlivet*, obtained a license, followed by many other Highland* distillers.

Liqueur

Whisky liqueurs are mixtures of whisky and complementary aromatic substances, notably herbs, honey, or even fruit. The exact origin of these liqueurs remains hazy. However, it is likely that they were created accidentally at the same time as the first whiskies. Herbs or honey were then used to smooth out the taste* of the young whisky, which was sometimes too dry, or too bitter.

Drambuie, the most famous Scottish whisky liqueur, was supposedly offered by Prince Charles Edward Stuart as a gift to one of his hosts in 1746. The two other great whisky nations, Ireland* and the United States*, have not been outdone in this field. The Irish equivalent of Drambuie is a liqueur known as Irish Mist. But Ireland is above all famous for Bailey's, a liqueur whose recipe includes cream. In the United States, Southern Comfort, made from bourbon*, aromatic herbs, and fruit (peaches, oranges) is also very highly regarded.

Those who sometimes find liqueurs excessively sweet, are advised to drink them "on the rocks" (with ice cubes). The combination* of a whisky liqueur and chocolate with a high cocoa content can also bring a moment of intense pleasure.

Right: Humphrey Bogart in *Casablanca*, 1943.

▪ LITERATURE AND CINEMA
Chandler, Hemingway, John Ford

It is very unfair to Ireland* and Scotland*, the spiritual homes of *uisge beatha**, but Humphrey Bogart, in the role of the private detective Philip Marlowe, certainly did more for whisky's image than all their writers and poets put together. It is to American literature and Hollywood that we owe our thanks for having introduced whisky into the Western imagination. There is not a single novel by Chandler, Faulkner, Fitzgerald, or Hemingway (to name but a few) in which whisky does not calm the existential angst of some character or other; heroes in John Ford's and Howard Hawks' movies never exude more virility than when knocking back a few swigs of vile saloon hooch.

But whisky is sometimes also the classic enemy of the hero: in the Billy Wilder movie *Poison*, and in John Sturges' *Gunfight at the OK Corral*, Ray Milland and Doc Holliday are men brought low by whisky. In John Cassavetes' *A Woman Under the Influence*, or Barbet Shroeder's *Barfly*, adapted from the book by Charles Bukowski, whisky is the catalyst for madness and human despair. Happily, not all authors portray alcohol in an unhappy light! In the movie *Designing Woman*, a comedy by Vincente Minelli, the story is built around a raging drunk hired by Gregory Peck to help him marry Lauren Bacall. In his novel entitled *Whisky Galore*—from which a movie of the same name was made—Sir Compton Mackenzie tells the story of a shipment of whisky washed up on the Isle of Todday in the Hebrides, which allows the inhabitants to regain their health and pride.

LLOYD GEORGE

Lloyd George (David)

Although whisky has always been heavily taxed*, one man can boast of having been its worst enemy: the Welshman, David Lloyd George (1863–1945).

In 1909, when he was Chancellor of the Exchequer, Lloyd George had a law voted in which aimed to raise whisky duties by thirty-three percent to finance his plan of social reforms. He made use of the First World War to increase repressive measures towards distilleries. Under pressure from him, the maximum alcohol by volume for a whisky was lowered from sixty percent to 37.5 percent.

Then in 1918, whisky exports were forbidden and whisky duties were doubled. Lloyd George went so far as to suggest absolute prohibition*, but unlike his American counterparts, he failed in his attempt to introduce it.

This legislation quickly put the majority of whisky companies in financial difficulties. Only DCL* was able to face up to this disastrous situation, by buying up distilleries and failing companies.

Lloyd George died in 1945 at the age of 82, and whisky, happily, still flows from the stills.

Portrait of David Lloyd George by Sir William Orpen (1878–1931). Private collection.

"Fortune! if thou'll but gie me still
Hale breeks, a scone, an' whisky gill,
An' rowth o' rhyme to rave at will,
Tak a' the rest,
An' deal't about as thy blind skill
Directs thee best."

Robert Burns, *Scotch Drink*

Lowlands

This region occupies the southern part of Scotland* (see map) and is marked out in the north by the Edinburgh-Greenock line, and in the south by the Cheviot Hills, the natural border with England. The countryside and pastures of this relatively flat area were an inspiration to the poet Robert Burns*. Sir Walter Scott, another very famous writer, spent several years here.

Though there were dozens of malt distilleries in the nineteenth century, only three still remain active these days; Auchentoshan, Glenkinchie, and Inverleven. Happily enough, other Lowlands malts are still available from independent bottlers*, among which the names of Bladnoch, Ladyburn, Littlemill, Rosebank, and Saint Magdalene are worth noting. These whiskies are packed full of fruitiness and are very light. If there is a logical path of discovery to be made through malt whiskies, those from the Lowlands should be at the very start. Peat* is rarely or only moderately used in making the whiskies which, apart from certain special vintages, mature quickly; a ten-year aging* in casks* is generally long enough. Several grain* distilleries have been established in the area, and almost all of their production is allocated to blenders*. The Lowlands also contain the two largest towns in Scotland: Glasgow, an industrial town in the west, and in the east, Edinburgh, a majestic town constructed on an old volcano.

74

■ MALT
100 percent malted barley whiskies

Malt is barley whose germination has been artificially induced (see Malting). The idea of the "pure malt" leads to a certain confusion since this description covers two different categories of whisky, both made from malt.

The first category is pure malts that come from one distillery alone: these are single malts*. Though they constitute the aristocracy of Scottish whisky, this term only started being used fairly recently. The name of the distillery is usually mentioned on the bottle's label*.

The second category consists of pure malts that come from a mixture of malts from different distilleries. The term "pure malt" is usually used in this case, but there are other possible titles, such as "vatted malt," "malt Scotch whisky," etc. The name of the distilleries is never mentioned on the label. The malts of this second type, though often overlooked these days, are no less interesting. They may be made from malts of the same area or from different areas. The famous company Gordon & Macphail offers a remarkable range of pure malts (vatted malts), the best known of which are: Highland Fusiliers, Old Elgin, Pride of Strathspey, and Pride of Islay*. One phrase sums the subject up perfectly: all single malts are pure malts, but not all pure malts are single malts.

Malt drying, Port Ellen malthouse. Isle of Islay, Scotland.

■ Malting

Malting consists in inducing germination in barley. The aim of this operation is to release the starch contained in the grain so that it can then be transformed into maltose (sugar) during mashing*.

The barley is plunged into a vat filled with the distillery's own water*, known as a "steep." Drained and spread out on a bare stone "malting floor," the barley is then stirred and turned over several times a day so that its germination is uniform. Depending on the region, this stage can last between eight and fifteen days. Experience is essential since it is by smelling and tasting the malting barley that the maltster decides the moment that germination should be stopped. To accomplish this, the "green malt" (for from now on it is known as malt*) is dried. Its moisture level at this stage is fifty percent and the starch has only partially been transformed into sugars. Drying takes place in a sort of oven, the "kiln." The fuels used are peat*, wood, coal, gas and even fuel oil, with certain distilleries using a mixture of these. During the "kilning," the grain should only be lightly toasted and brittle, and the temperature should not exceed 158° F (70° C). Traditionally, drying lasts between two and three days, by which time the barley's moisture level has gone down to three percent.

These days, few distilleries malt their own barley. Major malt-houses use mechanical methods, among which is the Saladin process, invented by a French engineer and used regularly since the 1960s.

The defenders of mechanization appreciate the more controlled, regular malting it allows. In these centers, malting only lasts seven days. Aside from barley, other grains* can be malted: after being ground, those used for making whiskies are pressure-cooked. As they are heated up, their cellulose covering dissolves, releasing the starch, and they are then ready for mashing*.

■ MANUFACTURE
Water, fire, and time

Whiskies are made from grain*. They can be made from barley alone or from a mixture of several different grains. The manufacture of pure malt* whiskies (barley alone) is carried out in five stages, each of which is equally important.

Barley, corn, and rye used to make Tennessee whiskey.

The first stage is malting*. This operation consists in making the grain germinate through humidification. A "green malt" is obtained which is then dried and ground into a thick flour known as "grist." Then follows the mashing*, whereby hot water is added, which produces a liquid called the "wort." By this stage, the starch contained in the malt has turned into fermentable sugars. When the selected yeasts start to work, the sugars ferment to become alcohol: the liquid obtained, the "wash," is eight percent alcohol by volume. Then it is the turn of distillation*: the wash or fermented liquid (which is now a type of beer) is boiled in a still to extract the alcohol from it. The resulting liquid leaves the still at around 68 percent alcohol by volume. Finally, the production cycle of pure malt is finished by aging* in oak casks*. The expression "water, fire, and time," to which "air" should perhaps be added, emphasizes the role played by the natural elements. These elements can only be brought together by humans, and a pure malt always reveals something of the people that produced it. It is in this sense that it becomes a sort of work of art.

To make blends*, malt whiskies (barley), and grain whiskies (maize, wheat, rye, etc.) are combined after distillation or at the bottling stage.

Mashing

Mashing, the second stage in a whisky's manufacture, transforms starch into sugars.

After malting* or "cooking" (according to whether it is barley or some other grain), the grain is ground into a thick flour, the "grist," then mixed with water* from the distillery's own spring, which has been heated to between 145 and 154 ° F (63°

residue of the grist, the "draff," is used for feeding local cattle. From the amount of wort produced, it is possible to estimate the volume of alcohol that will be obtained after distillation*. This is where the excisemen come in. In agreement with the distiller, they will fix a production quota that must be strictly obeyed under threat of fines.

Mashing in an industrial vat.

and 68° C). The mixture, which contains one-quarter grist to three-quarters water, is then poured into a vat equipped with rotating blades, the mash tun. Now the mashing starts: after several hours and under the effect of the hot water, the starch is transformed into maltose. The sugar-rich liquid which is obtained little by little during the mashing, the "wort," is run off into an intermediate vat, the "underback." So as to recover the remaining sugar in the grist, it is sprayed with water twice more. The new worts obtained are placed with the first batch and the whole lot is cooled to 73 ° F (23° C) in a chilling cabinet. A small quantity of the sugared liquid is preserved and used to start off the next mashing process. The

Medicinal

We know that the first monk distillers used *uisge beatha* * for massaging the painful limbs of working animals. Very soon afterwards, men started to adapt it to their own use, and not just for rubbing themselves down!

In 1505, in order to reserve alcohol for exclusively medical ends, the government of Edinburgh gave the distillation* monopoly to the guild of barber surgeons. In 1564, the famous chronicler, Holinshed, declared, tongue in cheek, that whisky stopped the spinal column from melting and the bones from breaking. Though at this time whisky was used for its sterilizing and analgesic power (especially against raging toothache), intensive studies

77

The medicinal
benefits of
whisky.

have since shown that the moderate consumption of whisky helps fight against cardiac troubles, dysentery, cholera, malaria, fatigue, depression, and other maladies. In the United States* during Prohibition*, six distilleries produced a so-called medicinal whiskey, available on prescription... Even nowadays, one hears the peat-flavored whiskies of the Isle of Islay* described as having a "taste of medicine." Maybe this gives substance to the theory that whisky really does have medicinal qualities.

in the country (see map). This distillation* complex makes whiskies from malted and non-malted barley. And, uniquely in the world, Midleton also produces single malts*, grain* whiskies, and blends*. To do

■ Midleton

Cask storage
at the Midleton
Distillery,
Ireland.

Situated in the south of Ireland* not far from Cork, the town of Midleton lends its name to the largest distillery

all of this it has two types of still*—pot stills in the purest Scottish style, and, more surprisingly for Ireland, Coffey* stills. Over 200 years ago, in May 1796, Marcus Lynch had a wool mill built on the site of the modern-day distillery. Round about 1820, the land was bought up by Lord Midleton, who then sold it on to his three brothers, James, Daniel, and Jeremiah Murphy. Forerunners in the field of industrial mergers, in 1867 they grouped together the distilleries of Cork (North Mall, The Watercourse, The Green, Daly) to create the Cork Distilleries Company.

Nothing changed up until 1966, when Cork Distilleries joined with its two main competitors, John Jameson* and John Power's* to create the Irish Distillers Group. The decision was then taken to concentrate all production in Midleton, and a new distillery was set up in 1975. The sole reminders of the past are the buildings of North Mall, which date from 1779. They house the blending operations of the highly prestigious Midleton Very Rare, the only vintage Irish whiskey. Midleton also produces the famous whiskeys Jameson, Green Spot, Power's, Paddy, Hewitts, Dunphys, Redbreast, and Tullamore Dew.

■ Packaging

Dimple is a blended Scotch* famous for its triangular bottle and its three indented sides. The design of this bottle has been preserved since 1893, when it was a leader in the area of packaging. More than a century later, marketing and design have revolutionized the whisky industry, especially the manufacture of containers.

Some blenders will stop at nothing to sell their product, trying to outdo each other in eye-catching bad taste and eccentricity. Take for example a decanter in the shape of a bell, or a stoneware bottle in the form of a monk, whose head acts as the bottle top.

Some less fanciful malt* bottles are made along cleaner lines, and can be valuable. An engraved crystal decanter containing a thirty-year-old Glenfiddich has a silver deer's head as a stopper, making this collector's malt highly expensive. The current trend is towards a plainer, more authentic style. The Classic Malts collection owes its considerable success since its launch in 1988 as much to the quality of the whisky as to the excellent design of the six bottles that make up the range. One thing is sure: packaging sells. Let us hope that the producers pay as much attention to the contents as to the container.

Dimple, John Haig Scotch Whisky, twelve years old.

Jack Daniel's Tennessee whiskey.

■ Peat

If you ask a specialist to recommend a peaty whisky they will almost certainly suggest one from the Isle of Islay*. They might also point you in the direction of certain Highland* whiskies such as Brora or even Longrow, a malt* from the Campbeltown* peninsula. Peat, compacted earth, is a thousand-

Cut in chunks from peat bogs, peat is used as a fuel for drying malt, which it permeates with its thick, dense smoke. The water* from the distilleries' springs takes on the flavor of the peat bogs which drain into them.

Peaty whiskies give off aromas of tarmac and diesel fuel. The flavor in the mouth is domi-

Peat fire for drying malt, Isle of Islay, Scotland.

year-old fossilized coal composed of plant material, mosses, leaves, and seaweed. In the north of Scotland* it is black, on Skye or Islay it is iodized and brown. It can also be found on the island of Hokkaido in Japan*, where it is lighter and has a less strong flavor.

nated by licorice and a very characteristic bouquet (see Vocabulary), closer to smoked tea than to the charred wood taste of a bourbon*. All it needs is one glass of very peaty Islay whisky such as Ardbeg, Laphroaig or Lagavulin to perfume a whole room.

■ POTEEN
The ancestor of whiskey

Of Irish origin, poteen (pronounced "potsheen"), produced by illicit distillers since the seventeenth century, has some claim to be the ancestor of Irish whiskey.

On Christmas Day 1661, the English introduced a tax* on every gallon of whiskey* produced; illicit distillation* of poteen in Ireland* dates from that day. More than a century later, the English government decided to raise taxes again to finance the wars against Napoleon. Illicit distillation then reached its peak despite the repressive tactics of the excisemen. It was, however, unable to resist the anti-alcohol lobby or survive the reconversion of many farmer distillers into law-abiding property owners.

In the beginning, poteen was simply a whiskey that had not been aged in cask*. The use of peat* speeded up the malt drying process. Then, with a view to increasing productivity, the illicit distillers started substituting potatoes for grain*, or using molasses or even apples to speed up the fermentation process.

The producers of this type of poteen are very rare nowadays. However, those who hanker for the past can console themselves with a modern version of poteen, Bunratty Potcheen, whose production has recently been legalized in Ireland.

Following double page: whisky bottling. Maker's Mark Distillery. Loretto, Kentucky, USA.

Irish still, Sir David Wilkie (1785–1841). National Gallery, Edinburgh.

Power (John)

In 1976 the John's Lane Distillery closed down completely. It was at this distillery that the famous Irish whiskey, John Power's, had been made for almost two hundred years. The whiskey* itself survived, but from then on it was produced at Midleton*. Nowadays all that remains of this glorious past are some ruins and three giant stills*.

It all began in 1791, when James Power decided to transform his inn into a distillery. His son John helped him to build up the business which prospered from 1823 onwards, the year taxes* were lowered and the whisky laws were liberalized. Power's success was beneficial to the whole region of Dublin. In recognition of his contribution to the city, he was first made a knight and then, later on, Mayor of Dublin.

In 1871, the distillery was rebuilt and became one of the city's main attractions. Power deserved success as much for the quality of his whiskey as for his business spirit. He was one of the first to market his products commercially in many different forms (see Packaging), in particular as whiskey miniatures called "Baby Power's." It was also at this time that the gold-lettered label*, the symbol of the brand, was created. At this time the whiskey, made from a mixture of malted and non-malted barley, was distilled in traditional pot stills*. Then, at the beginning of the 1950s, Power's adopted the more economical process of continuous distillation. Production was in effect relaunched after Prohibition* and the war years. Despite this, the distillery found itself in difficulties and had to join its two main competitors, John

Jameson & Son and the Cork Distilleries Company to form Irish Distillers. Ten years later, the famous Dublin distillery closed its doors for the last time.

Preservation

Unlike wine, whiskey does not change after it has been bottled. However, it is advisable to take some precautions to assure its longevity. The first rule to respect is to keep whisky bottles upright so that the alcohol is not in contact with the cork. It should also be kept away from all sources of heat in order to avoid drying out the cork, which would allow air to get into the bottle. One question which is often asked, and over which whisky lovers are divided, concerns whether or not to use a decanter. From an aesthetic point of view, it is undeniable that in a decanter the different shades of color* of a whisky can be seen to their best advantage. Moreover, the decanter is part of the ceremony, and adds significance to the gesture of inviting someone to have a whisky. Purists think that the use of a decanter has the effect of making the whisky harder by overexposing it to the surrounding air. A young whisky will withstand a decanter less well than an old whisky, which has already undergone oxidization during years of aging* in cask*.

Keeping a young whisky in a bottle and putting an old whisky in a decanter combines aesthetic pleasure with the joy of tasting*.

Prohibition

On January 17, 1920, Prohibition came into force in the United States*. A century earlier, in 1826, the city of Boston

had seen the creation of the American Temperance Society. In the beginning, this movement advocated only moderation rather than abstinence. However, between 1865 and 1900, the huge growth of the whiskey* industry made its opponents more radical; they called for a total ban on alcohol consumption on American territory. A society bluntly named the "Anti-Saloon League" was created in 1893. In 1909, twenty states had already adopted some form of Prohibition, some stricter than others. Faced with this hardening of attitudes, the whiskey industry found new methods of selling, such as mail-order sales, which were not subject to legislation. The First World War was a fresh blow to the whiskey industry. In order to preserve grain* reserves, the federal government made alcohol distillation* illegal. After the war, production started up again in a small way, but on January 17, 1920, the Volstead Act introduced nationwide Prohibition. A tombstone was erected in Meridian (Connecticut) to the memory of John Barleycorn, the famous character created by the poet Robert Burns*. On it these words can be read: "In memoriam John Barleycorn. Born B.C. Died Jan. 16, 1920. Resurrection?"
However, for some of the population at least, alcohol continued to flow freely in speakeasies. Mobsters and bootleggers* profited greatly from this period, amassing huge personal fortunes. Taken aback by the new law, some distilleries continued to produce whiskey for medicinal* purposes, which was dispensed on prescription in pharmacies.

Mob warfare during the Prohibition era in the USA.

Under pressure from the powerful families and associations of the fight against Prohibition, the law was finally repealed thirteen years later, on December 5, 1933 at 5.32 p.m. exactly. Runaway crime and the serious fall in income for the State and for farmers who had lost an important market were given as reasons for this.
But Prohibition had led to the dismantling of the whiskey industry: of seventeen distilleries registered in Kentucky* before 1920, only seven started to produce again after 1933.

■ Rye

When thinking of American whiskeys*, it is bourbons* and Tennessee* whiskies that spring to mind. However there is a third, rye whiskey, though it is

rarely produced nowadays. This least well known of whiskeys is also the oldest. The first Irish and Scottish settlers produced a rye-based alcohol from the end of the seventeenth century onwards. Rye, imported from Northern Europe, grew easily on the poor soil of Pennsylvania and Maryland. Rye whiskey

Advertisement for Harvard pure rye whiskey.

produced in the United States* is made from a mixture of grains containing a minimum of 51 percent rye. It is a straight whiskey: it is not cut with a neutral alcohol and after distillation* it is never more than 80 percent proof. Aged for a minimum of two years in new oak casks* to gain the right to be called "rye," it is then bottled at 40 percent proof or higher. American rye should not be confused with its Canadian cousin. More widely known, Canadian rye is generally made from a mixture of straight rye whisky and grain alcohol. Nowadays, the terms "Canadian whisky," "rye whisky," or simply "rye" all refer to the same type of whisky.

SAINT PATRICK

Saint Patrick.
Tiepolo, 1746.
Museo Civico,
Padua.

SAINT PATRICK
The father of whisky

On March 17 every year, Irish people around the world carry on the tradition of celebrating St. Patrick's Day. In certain cities, such as New York, gigantic parades are organized to mark the occasion.

The story begins in 432 A.D., when a monk, fresh from evangelical work in the Middle East, went to Ireland to convert the population to Christianity. Saint Patrick was keenly interested in the distillation* techniques used

for the production of perfume, and it was with a perfect knowledge of this blossoming art that he installed himself in County Wicklow. The production of *uisge beatha** was to develop from this point on, finally culminating in whiskey*.

Rightly or wrongly, the Irish claim the paternity of whisky, to the great displeasure of their Scottish cousins. The Scots console themselves with the fact that Saint Patrick was born in Scotland!

Scotch

The Scots, an Irish tribe who were to give their name to Scotland, were first heard of in 500 A.D. It was in 1034, when they took possession of almost the whole country, that the Kingdom of Scotland* was born. The first reference to Scotch whisky dates back to 1494. In that year, a monk, John Corr, bought eight "bolls" of barley (around 1,100 pounds/500 kilos) to be made into *uisge beatha**. Scotch whisky had been born.

The definition of Scotch was confirmed for the first time by a royal commission in 1908. Then in 1988 the Scotch Whisky Act was voted in. Under the terms of this law, in order to use the description "Scotch," whisky has to be

made from a mixture of water*, malt*, and, if necessary, other types of grain*, transformed into a fermented mash* by the addition of yeasts. It must be produced and distilled in Scotland and have an alcohol content no higher than 94.8 percent. Finally it must age in oak casks* for a minimum of three years before being bottled at a strength no lower than forty percent. (In Scotland this law allows the use of caramel, which influences the color more than the taste).

These days, the term "Scotch" is used less and less to identify Scottish whiskies. More popular are the terms "blends*," "pure malts*," "single malts*," and "single grains*," but they all refer to whiskies that are made in Scotland.

Ruskin Spear,
*Inside the
Hop Poles Pub.*
Taylor Gallery,
London.

88

■ SCOTLAND

Whisky is to Scotland what tea is to China, or wine is to France. Just like Scotland, it possesses a unique and multi-faceted personality. The splendors of the lakes and mountains, the dryness of certain parts of the north, the silence of the southern countryside, and the picturesque character of the peat-covered islands, are what give Scotland and Scotch* their originality.

It is unclear where distillation* first began. Some people attribute its introduction to the first Christian monks from Ireland, who came ashore on the west coast in the sixth century; others are convinced it goes back as far as 300 B.C., when the country was dominated by a tribe called the Picts. The only thing that is certain is that the first written reference to the manufacture of whisky in Scotland dates back to 1494.

Even though it had been illicitly distilled for centuries, it was not until the nineteenth century that Scotch really took off. The appearance of the first great blended* brands, and the commercial dynamism of some of the independent bottlers* allowed Scotch to assert its supremacy, especially over its Irish rival. The success gained by blended Scotch rapidly spread beyond the borders of the United Kingdom despite periods of successive crises which hit Scotland and the rest of the world in the first half of the nineteenth century.

Above left: A bottle of Tamnavulin whisky.
Above: Tormore Distillery. Highlands, Speyside.

As for the pure malts*, the other great family of Scottish whiskies, although they originate from when whisky was first made in Scotland, they only really made their appearance on the market towards the end of the 1960s. More characteristic than blends, in the eyes of whisky buffs they are the most noble of all whiskies.

Malt distilleries are scattered throughout Scotland. This largely explains the diversity of tastes* and aromas* of the whiskies they produce, so marked are the geological and climatic differences between regions. Even when two neighboring distilleries take their water* from the same spring or use the same barley—as is the case at Speyside*—their malts are different.

It is to this richness and diversity that Scotch owes its privileged place in the world of whiskies. Some people do not hesitate to declare that Scotland is *the* country of whisky.

SINGLE CASK

Single cask

Single casks (Scottish) and single barrels (American) are not only the product of one sole distillery, but also of one sole cask*. Single casks are to the single malts of Scotland what single barrels are to the straight whiskeys of the United States. Single casks are generally available from independent bottlers*. Two distinct signs allow one to identify them—the distillation* date and the bottling date, which appear on the label*. Often a cask* number and a bottle number are also given.

The quality of single casks owes more to chance than to careful selection, since independent bottlers* are becoming more and more dependent on the producers to supply them with casks. It is, therefore, even more important than usual to select them meticulously. Sometimes, exceptional casks allow one to discover unique varieties of whisky: a whisky that has traditionally been aged in a bourbon* cask may, for example, be available in a version aged in a sherry cask.

As for single barrels, the selection of barrels is entirely dependent on the producer. It is he or she who decides to set apart some barrels, considered better than the others, and to put them to one side in the warehouse to age*. As they have a more limited distribution than single casks, they deserve special attention.

Single malt

Although this is by no means the case any longer, all Scottish whiskies were originally single malts.

These days such whiskies are the most prized by whisky buffs. Some of them have

even become real cult objects. Single malts are made solely from malted barley, and come from one distillery alone. Pot stills* are used to distil the whisky twice or, in some cases, three times. Glenturret, the oldest malt* distillery, was created in 1772.

Until the middle of the twentieth century, the majority of single malts made were intended for blends. Before this, only a few independent bottlers*, notably Gordon & Macphail at Elgin, were wise enough to build up stocks of single malts, which largely contributed to their growing popularity.

At the beginning of the 1970s, the Glenfiddich Distillery launched the first commercial single malt. However, it was not until the end of the 1980s and the introduction of a range of six whiskies named the Classic Malts that single malt whiskies really took off.

Spread out among four regions of Scotland*, single malts offer major differences in character. In southern Scotland are the Lowlands*, with light malts; in the south-west is the Campbeltown* peninsula with its famous Springbank Distillery; then there is the Isle of Islay*, whose typical malts are intensely peaty; and in the north-east the vast Highlands* region, which includes the Orkney islands, the Hebrides, and Speyside*. Today 108 distilleries are in working order, of which only eighty are still producing. Ireland* offers two single malts: Bushmills*, a ten-year-old malt, and Tyrconnel.

Right: Sacks of malt waiting to be made into whisky.

92

The Marx Brothers in *A Night at the Opera*, 1935.

Sociability

Whisky has always been a source of conviviality, although the way in which it is drunk has changed a lot over time. Originally, partly because it was distilled illicitly, whisky contributed to forging the national identity of the country in which it was produced. *Uisge beatha** was distilled and drunk for the pleasure of meeting up over a glass, but also in reaction against the heavy taxes* imposed by the powers that be. Later when the first Irish and Scottish colonists arrived in the immense territories that were to become the United States* and Canada*, they started producing whisky straight away, as a means of carrying on the tradition and the spirit of the clan*.

At the end of the nineteenth century, the considerable expansion of the great blended* brands was to change consumption* habits again. Due to their success in London high society, these whiskies were introduced into private clubs*. Though whisky remained a fundamental source of conviviality, it also took on a more fashionable aspect. In the 1950s and 1960s, whilst keeping its image as a chic pre-dinner drink, whisky became the essential, universally known alcoholic beverage.

For several years, whisky has been the object of a genuine craze among a growing number of enthusiasts. Normal drinking sometimes becomes a real tasting* session, and friends invite each other round to spend time enjoying a venerable single malt*, or an old bourbon*.

Sour mash

You may already have been surprised to notice a bottle of Kentucky* bourbon marked with the term "sour mash," also known as "setback" or "backset," though other whiskey* bottles from the same source do not mention it.

Do sour mash whiskeys have something extra? Not at all. For nowadays all Kentucky bourbons as well as all Tennessee* and rye whiskeys are sour mash whiskeys. If this fact is mentioned, it is only for effect.

In practical terms, "sour mash" is an element used in the manufacture of these types of whiskey. It refers to a residue from the bottom of the still* that is added when the water* and cereals are mashed, making up nearly twenty-five percent of the mix. Very acidic, it helps to avoid bacterial contamination and undesirable yeasts. This is why it is best for all whiskies to be sour mash!

Drugstore specializing in whisky. Edinburgh, Scotland.

Testing a
four-year-old
whiskey before
bottling (USA)

Specialist

At the end of the 1950s, there were very few countries where one could find more than twenty or so whiskies from around the world. Forty odd years later, there are hundreds of whiskies, including the numerous blended* brands and those bottled by independent merchants. Faced with this huge flood of brands and labels*, the consumer is increasingly at a loss; specialist departments in superstores are crammed full, as whisky has now become such a fashionable drink. Informed advice is more vital than ever;

nothing can replace the human touch when it comes down to buying a bottle of whisky. Luckily there are specialists (see Buyer's Guide), who not only make recommendations but also know the whiskies they sell inside out. They are able to guide the beginner as well as the knowledgeable whisky lover. In addition to the advice they give, they can provide some very rare bottles, for example whiskies that come from distilleries that have been closed for a long time, or vintages from the 1940s. The specialist will give you access to a world of whisky which contains hitherto unsuspected treasures.

■ Speyside

"The Golden Triangle" is the nickname given to Speyside (see map), in the heart of the Highlands*, due to its high concentration of distilleries, set in an area that stretches from Elgin in the west, to Banff in the east, and Dufftown in the south.

The Spey
(Speyside,
Scotland)

Distillation of *uisge* beatha. Plate taken from the *Encyclopedia*

However, not all Speyside whiskies come from immediately around the river Spey. This river ends at the North Sea and is joined along its way by the Livet, the Fiddich, and the Avon rivers, famous names that are bywords for quality. The Speyside malts* have great prestige, and their diversity leads to very interesting tasting* experiences. It is in this region that the first Highlands* distillery to have been granted a license* is found, Glenlivet*, which gives its name to a style of whisky. It was also a Speyside whisky, Glenfiddich, which popularized pure malts* in the beginning of the 1970s. The other well-known distilleries are: Macallan, famous for aging* its whiskies in sherry casks*; Glenfarclas, sought after for its powerful

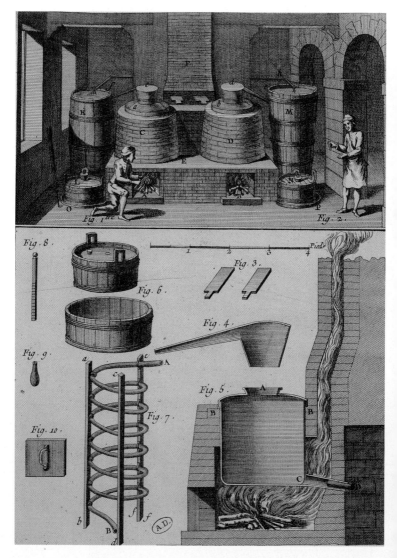

malt; Glendronach and its characteristic malts; Strathisla and its classic whiskies; Balvenie and its subtle, traditional malt; Mortlach, whose whisky is pear-flavored; Aberlour; Glen Grant; Knockando; Linkwood; Longmore; and many others.

Speyside whiskies are generally mellow, marked by the sweetness of the malt and the delicate peaty* accents.

■ Spirits

Spirits are often confused with alcoholic drinks. All spirits are alcoholic drinks, but not all alcoholic drinks are spirits.

A spirit is the result of a distillation, whatever the raw material used may be: grains* for whisky, grapes for cognac or armagnac, apples for calvados. On the other hand, beer, champagne, and wine, which are rarely more than 15 percent ABV, are alcoholic drinks. It is distillation* that allows the alcohol content to be increased; it goes from four percent to twenty percent for alcoholic drinks, to sixty percent and more for spirits.

Another characteristic of spirits is that once bottled they do not change, which is not the case with wines or with most port wines. Other famous spirits are vodka, gin, aniseed drinks, fruit-based eau de vie (brandy), and others in the brandy family. Though vodka may be drunk in more quantities than any other spirit, whisky can be found in a larger number of countries.

■ Still

The dictionary gives the following definition of a still: "Distilling apparatus." More precisely, the still is used for turning the liquid created by fermentation* into alcohol, by heating and condensation. Stills can be used to produce perfumes and make-up, notably kohl (which forms part of the word alcohol—"Al kohl"). Two types of still are used for the production of whisky: the pot still (the oldest), and the patent still or Coffey still, perfected in the nineteenth century by Aeneas Coffey*. The first is used for non-continuous distillation* (it has to be stopped for long cleaning operations between each vatful), the second for continuous distillation (it keeps working as long as it is kept supplied with fermented grain* and steam).

The copper pot stills are used for pure malts* and certain Irish whiskeys. They remind one of huge kettles mounted on a long swan-neck in which alcohol vapors rise up, and are then condensed as they pass through a coil that plunges into a cooling compartment. They come in different shapes and sizes according to the distillery: long, narrow stills in principle produce lighter whiskies than stills with a large diameter. When one part of a still is defective or worn out, it is replaced by an identical part with all its bumps and hollows: custom states that, if even slightly altered, it will not produce exactly the same whisky. The second type of still, the Coffey or patent still, is used for grain whiskies (maize, rye*, mixtures of barley, and other grains). It is made up of two copper columns, the analyzer and the rectifier, divided into chambers by a series of perforated platforms. The alcohol is made when the vapor—which circulates continuously in the analyzer and rectifier—comes into contact with the liquid. On average, this type of still produces sixteen times more whisky in a year than a traditional pot still.

Following double page: stills at the Glenfiddich Distillery in Dufftown (Speyside, Scotland)

Blender sniffing
whisky samples
for blending,
Dewar's,
Scotland.

■ Taste

Traditions and laws are at the root of the individual whisky tastes of each producing country. Canadian whisky is marked by its fruitiness, lightness, and mellowness; it also has a slightly bitter taste because of the large amount of rye* it contains. In the United States*, whiskeys are characterized by a rich body, a fruity sweetness, and intense woody tones, due to being aged in brand new casks* which have been thoroughly charred inside. They are also often evocative of leather. Japanese whisky, although inspired by Scottish whisky, nonetheless has its own personality, characterized by a light fruitiness, smoky tones, and a slight dryness at the end of the mouth. Irish whiskey* has an attractive firmness, and a pronounced fruitiness evocative of red fruits. Scotland* produces whiskies that differ a great deal from one region to another; it is the country that offers the greatest diversity of tastes. From light and fruity, to iodized and peaty*, the tasting range is infinite, as is the vast vocabulary* used to describe it.

The taste of a whisky is traditionally perceived in four major parts: the attack in the mouth, the middle of the mouth, the end of the mouth, and the finish. To this one must add a fifth stage, which centers more around smell than taste: several minutes after having drunk a whisky, the drinker has a sense of the flavor returning, sometimes very different from what it was before. This is a phenomenon called retro-olfaction. The list of the different tastes experienced is very long. Here is a brief sample: almond, aniseed, berries, toffee, chocolate, clove, currant, malt, hazelnut, peach, pear, licorice, peat, clover, and even violet.

■ TASTING
A special moment

Without being too solemn about it, a certain amount of ceremony adds to the pleasure of this special moment. The tasting begins with an examination of the whisky's color*. Then follows the analysis by smell; add a little still water to the whisky so that the aroma* can develop. A narrow, slightly tapered glass* that is large enough to permit this helps one to savor the scent. The opposite of wine, one should not swirl one's glass in order to appreciate the aromatic qualities of a whisky. The first sniff brings out the dominant aromas, then by inhaling more deeply all the complexity of smell is revealed.

Finally, the moment of tasting the whisky arrives. Its ideal temperature is between 64 and 68 ° F (18° and 20° C). If colder than this, the temperature will make the smell very faint, whilst a temperature that is too high makes the alcohol stand out. The whisky should be held in the mouth for a few moments so as to fill the palate with the different tastes. The first impression is of the primary tastes (sugar, salt, acid, bitter). Then, progressively, the flavors of fruit, of flower, of spice will appear. The final impression can be short, or last for several minutes.

When should whisky be drunk, and what can be mixed with it? Everything depends on the whisky. Light and fruity whiskies, if diluted with a little water, make excellent pre-dinner drinks. Peaty whiskies, aged in sherry casks*, great bourbons*, and especially cask strength* whiskies are recommended for the end of a meal. Drinking whisky "on the rocks" masks its flavor as the ice inhibits the aroma from emerging. Whisky should be drunk without ice in order to enjoy it thoroughly.

▬ Tax

From very early on whisky has been important for governments, who see it as an inexhaustible source of revenue to finance wars and national debts. The first whisky tax dates back to 1644, and was imposed by the Scottish parliament to finance its war effort against the British. Then it was the turn of the English, who, to assert their authority, levied a tax on malt*. A veritable whisky war followed, which ended in 1823 when the legislation on whisky was relaxed. The excisemen were then ordered to oversee the quality and the quantity of the whisky produced by the distillers, on behalf of the government.

The same thing happened in America at the same time. A tax decreed by George Washington's government in 1791 brought about the exodus of thousands of distiller farmers to the west, to Kentucky*, Tennessee*, and Indiana, these states not yet being a part of the United States*. In 1920 this tax disappeared along with whisky itself, due to Prohibition*.

Caricature illustrating the rises in whiskey taxes, from *The Chicago Tribune.*

TENNESSEE

Nowadays whisky is doubly taxed. As well as the traditional VAT (Value Added Tax), there is a specific tax on alcoholic beverages: the duty is collected by Customs and based on the volume of pure alcohol. Strangely enough, Scotland*, the greatest whisky producer, is one of the countries with the highest duties.

■ Tennessee

When the first European settlers arrived in America, the territory called "Tanasie," an area crossed by many rivers and streams, was populated by Cherokee Indians. Nowadays it is known as Tennessee. Bordered by Kentucky*, North Carolina, and Mississippi, Tennessee was colonized by Irish immigrants fleeing the eastern states when the first whisky taxes* were introduced. Nicknamed the "Volunteer State," it owes its reputation to the bravery of its inhabitants in their fight against the English. Davy Crocket, a prime example, was one of the state's most famous inhabitants. Tennessee was also the scene of vicious confrontations during the American Civil War (1861–1865).

These days, this modern state has preserved the tradition of making Tennessee whiskey*. Made from a mixture of grains*, by law it must contain at least fifty-one percent of the same grain; maize is used most commonly, but is not obligatory. Almost all Tennessee whiskies are both sour mash*, and straight whiskeys. The thing that sets Tennessee whiskies apart from bourbon* or rye*, is the filtering process, carried out through a thick layer of charcoal. Known as the Lincoln County Process, or *charcoal mellowing*, this way of filtering was supposedly invented by Alfred Eaton in around 1825. It was only in 1941 that the federal government recognized Tennessee whiskey as distinct from bourbon. Nowadays, only two distilleries remain active: the famous Jack Daniel*, and George Dickel.

■ Uisge beatha

Coming from the Gaelic, the language of the ancient Celts, the terms *uisge beatha*, *uisce beatha*, or *usquebaugh* mean "water of life." Outside Ireland* and the Scottish Highlands*, it is the Latin term *aqua vitae* that was originally used to identify local spirits. It is the Latin expression that is used in the first written reference to whisky, in 1494.

Three centuries earlier the English, who had invaded Ireland, discovered this drink which was first used for medicinal* ends and whose name they had huge difficulty in pronouncing. This is the generally accepted origin of the distortion of the name *uisge beatha* into "whisky." The word *uisge* was mentioned in writing for the first time in

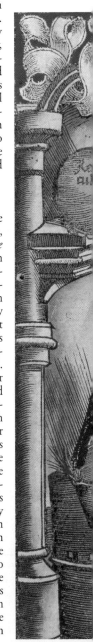

1618 at the funeral of a chief of a Highlands* clan. By a linguistic slide it became *uisce* then *fuisce*, and finally "whisky." Strangely enough, the expression *uisge beatha* has become very fashionable nowadays, largely due to the current enthusiasm for Celtic culture.

Still, Hieronymus Braunschweig, 1519. British Library, London.

The history of the United States is closely linked to that of its whiskeys. The first recorded distillations* date back to 1640, a mere 33 years after the arrival of the English colonists at Jamestown (Virginia).

The successive famines that hit Ireland* and Scotland* at the beginning of the eighteenth century led to a mass exodus to America. The immigrants did not forget to bring the little stills* that they used to produce *uisge beatha*. Soon the states of Pennsylvania, Maryland, and Virginia became famous for their rye-based drink, Monongahela, named after a river that crosses these states. Next, bourbon*, a whiskey named after a county in Kentucky* and Tennessee whiskey*, both made from maize, were to revolutionize the history of American whiskey.

After the Civil War (1861–1865), the entrepreneurial spirit of distillers such as Jack Daniel*, Jim Beam, and George Dickel gave birth to a veritable whiskey industry, which then suffered due to Prohibition* and the First World War.

Paradoxically, one of the consequences of the Second World War was the relaunch of the moribund American whiskey industry. Whiskey was exported to American soldiers stationed in Europe and Asia. This whiskey, immortalized by Westerns (see Literature and Cinema), then started to forge an identity for itself.

These days, in spite of everything, it is still suffering from a lack of recognition of its special qualities. The recent development of superior quality whiskeys, small batch and single barrel whiskeys (see Single Casks*) may perhaps provide the long-awaited kick-start for real success.

American whiskey is sometimes condemned for its strong taste* of caramel, whose origin is somewhat suspect—unlike in Scotland* or Ireland* the use of caramel is prohibited in the United States. Aside from the persistent flavors of caramel and wood, there are American whiskeys that have a wide range of scents and tastes. Their characteristic flavors are fruit (banana, lemon, blueberry, peach, orange); nut (walnut, hazelnut, cashew nut); spices (cinnamon, clove); and sometimes even tobacco (nicotine, cigars).

Above: A bottle of Jack Daniel's Tennessee whiskey.
Left: Maker's Mark Distillery. Loretto, Kentucky.

Usher (Andrew)

Andrew Usher was something of a trailblazer in his time. The exclusive agent for the Glenlivet* Distillery in the 1840s, he realized before anyone else how much whisky would be improved by prolonged aging* in casks*. Subsequently he took an interest in blending whiskies from different distilleries or of different ages, a practice that certain independent bottlers* had already experimented with rather haphazardly. He, however, adopted an empirical approach. Taking the example of cognac producers, he made his aim the creation of a blend that would be better than its various constituents. He christened his first blend Old Vatted Glenlivet. It was a mixture composed exclusively of single malts*, among which was The Glenlivet.

In 1853, Usher created the first modern blend*. He brought together a grain* alcohol from a patent still and a pure malt from the Highlands*, which he thought was too bitter to be marketed as it was. Usher thus demonstrated the huge potential of the still invented twenty years earlier by Aeneas Coffey*; he had succeeded in harmonizing the strength of a pure malt and the lightness of a grain alcohol. The characteristic taste of this blended whisky resembled the Lowland* malts, at the time highly prized by the English. From then on blends really took off.

The age of Usher was also the time when the great whisky companies, in particular DCL*, were created.

Andrew Usher.

Vocabulary

The vocabulary used for the description of whisky is both objective and subjective. The objective point of view is based on a careful translation of the sensations received through the eye, the nose, and the mouth. As for the subjective, this is where sensations unique to the individual come in—they invite a poetic, lyrical, mysterious, and even humorous journey.

Following the example of wines and other alcoholic beverages, whisky has seen its vocabulary increase considerably in the last twenty-five years or so. It is interesting to note that there are several different levels of language. The beginner will simply say a whisky is "good," the enthusiast will evoke subtle differences of peat* or sherry, the well-informed whisky buff will talk of fresh peat and an iodized perfume due to the distillery's microclimate.

The writer James Darwen, himself a great connoisseur, perfectly masters the technical language. He enlivens it with a humor that is sometimes disconcerting when, for example, he says he feels ready to "strangle seals" after sampling an Ardbeg, a very characteristic single malt* from the Isle of Islay*.

Walker (Hiram)

Ironically enough, the father of Canadian whisky was American. Hiram Walker (1816–1899) was born in Douglas, Massachusetts. At the age of twenty-two, he left home for the booming town of Detroit. In 1858, having made a fortune in the grain and vinegar business, he decided to build his own production unit including a distillery and a mill. Due to the anti-alcohol laws in Michigan, he settled in Canada*, near the town of Windsor.

After a very short time, Walker started to make a light and fruity style of whisky, the most perfect example of which was Canadian Club, a brand created in 1884. Its success was considerable, to the extent that it was widely imitated. Walker doggedly pursued the makers of these imitations, going so far as to use huge posters to denounce their activities.

At the same time, he put in place a series of major social measures: he built houses for his employees, a school, a church, a rail track, a town hall, and so on. In this way a town was born, and christened, in all modesty, "Walkerville."

By the time he died, in 1899, Hiram Walker had become one of the main whisky producers in North America. His son and grandson ran the business until 1926, when they sold it to Goodheram & Worts. Subsequently, the Hiram Walker group set up in Scotland*, buying the well-known blended* brand Ballantine's. Nowadays, Hiram Walker is the spirits subsidiary of the British group, Allied Domecq.

Hiram Walker.

■ **WATER**
The source of whisky

Water, fire, and time… the three essential elements for the manufacture of whisky. However, the most important of these is undoubtedly water. The setting up of distilleries is very closely linked to the presence of a source of water: a river, a stream, even a waterfall for certain distilleries situated at the foot of a mountain.

Water is first used for the germination of malt (see Malting). It is then used in the composition of the whisky itself, in the proportion of three-quarters water to a quarter grain*. Lastly, water is used to reduce the alcoholic strength of the whisky before it is bottled.

The nature of the water has a direct influence on the quality of the whisky produced. The light, peaty water used on the Scottish Isle of Islay* gives rise to rather heavy whiskies. Conversely, the crystal-clear water of Speyside* and the Northern Highlands* produces light whiskies. Naturally, Scotland* does not have the monopoly on quality of water. Part of the reason why Kentucky* was chosen more than two centuries ago as bourbon-making country was for the purity of its water. In Japan*, in the area around Kyoto, the Yamazaki valley, whose original name *Minaseno* means "source of water," is known for its pure water, which is naturally filtered through the granite rocks of Kai-Komagatake, the sacred mountain. It is in this valley that the best Japanese whiskies are produced.

Following double page: mountain stream near Cluanie Bridge, Highlands, Scotland.

■ WHISKEY
The Irish take pride in the extra "e"

The word "whiskey" comes from the corruption of the Gaelic term *uisge beatha** after the English invasion of Ireland, in around 1170. The Scottish, however, see this as the origin of their word—"whisky" without an "e." This is a never-ending debate between the two nations.

In practice, the use of the term "whiskey" comes from the Irish desire to differentiate their product from that of the Scots. According to Michael Jackson, a British writer specializing in beer and whisky, the term was originally only used in the city of Dublin, the stronghold of Irish whiskey. Then in the nineteenth century, its use developed and became more generalized.

Bottling of Old Times Whiskey at the beginning of the twentieth century. Kentucky, USA.

At that time, American whiskeys started to appear. In tribute to their mother country, the descendants of Irish immigrants christened the alcohol from their first distillations "whiskey." However, the term "whiskey" is not compulsory in the United States*, and the Maker's Mark, Old Forester, and Early Times bourbons* have opted for the Scottish word "whisky."

112

SPECIALIST STORES

Cadenhead's Whisky Shop
172 Canongate
Edinburgh EH8 8DF
Scotland
Tel.: 0131 556 5864

D & M Wine and Liquor
2200 Fillmore Street
San Francisco, CA 94102
USA
Tel.: (415) 346-1325

Gordon & Macphail
58-60 South Street
Elgin IV30 1JX
Scotland
Tel.: 01343 545 110

Hart Brothers
85 Springkell Ave
Glasgow G41 4EJ
Scotland
Tel.: 0141 427 6974

Loch Fyne Whisky
Inverary
Argyll PA32 8UD
Scotland
Tel.: 01499 302 219

La Maison du Whisky
20 rue d'Anjou
75008 Paris
France
Tel.: 01 42 65 03 16
www.maisonduwhisky.fr

Milroy's
3 Greek Street
London WIV 6NX
England
Tel.: 0207 437 2385

Park Avenue Liquors
292 Madison Avenue
New York, NY 10017
USA
Tel.: (212) 685-2442

Royal Mile Whiskies
379 High Street
Edinburgh EH1 1PW
Scotland
Tel.: 0131 225 3383

Vintage House
42 Old Compton Street
London WIV 6LR
England
Tel.: 0207 437 2592

CLUBS

The Scotch Malt Whisky
Society
87 Giles Street
Edinburgh
Scotland
Tel.: 0131 554 3451
www.smws.com

The Scotch Malt Whisky
Society (United States)
4604 North Hiatus Rd
Sunrise, FL 33326
USA
Tel.: (954) 749-2440
www.smwsa.com

The Keepers of the Quaich
Burke Lodge
20 London End
Beaconsfield
Bucks HP9 2JH
England
Tel.: 01494 670 035

Mini Bottle Club
Charfield House
Burnetts Lane
Horton Heath
Hants S050 7DG
England
Mini_Bottle_Club@
compuserve.com

The Kentucky
Bourbon Circle
P.O. Box 1
Clermont, KY 40110-9980
USA
Tel.: 1-800-6KB-CIRCLE

WHISKY AND BOURBON TOURS

Many distilleries are open for visits. Here is a brief selection. You are advised to telephone ahead and check opening hours.

United States

George Dickel
Cascade Hollow Road
Tullahoma, TN 37388
Tel.: (615) 857-3124

Heaven Hill
1064 Loretto Rd
Bardstown, KY 40004
Tel.: (502) 348-3921

Jack Daniel Barrelhouse
280 Lynchburg Hwy
Lynchburg, TN 37352
Tel.: (931) 759-4221
www.jackdaniel.com

Jim Beam
149 Happy Hollow Rd
Clermont, KY 40110
Tel.: (502) 543-9877
www.jimbeam.com

Maker's Mark
3350 Burks Springs Rd
Loretto, KY 40037
Tel.: (502) 865-2099

Scotland

Arran Distillery
Lochranza
Arran, Argyll KA27 8HJ
Tel.: 01770 830 264

Dallas Dhu Historic Distillery
Mannachie Road
Forres IV36 2RR
Morayshire
Tel.: 01309 676 548

Distillery Destinations Ltd.
304 Albert Drive
Glasgow G41 5RS
Tel.: 0141 429 0762
www.whisky-tours.com
Organizes tours to most
Scottish distilleries.

Canada

Canadian Club Distillery
2072 Riverside Drive East
Windsor, ON N8Y 4S5
Tel.: (519) 254-5171

Ireland

Old Jameson Distillery
Bow Street
Smithfield Village
Dublin 7
Tel.: 1 807 2355

Locke's Distillery
Kilbeggan, Co. Westmeath
Tel.: 0 506 32134

S E L E C T M A L T S

SCOTTISH MALTS * Inactive ** No longer producing

	Distilleries	Region	Nose principal notes	Flavor principal notes	Before a meal (B) After a meal (A)
1.	Aberfeldy	Southern Highlands	Heather/Peat	Barley/Peat	A
2.	Aberlour	Speyside	Spicy/Hazelnut	Spicy/Caramel	A
3.	Allt-A-Bhainne	Speyside	Peat/Floral	Spicy	B
4.	Ardbeg*	Isle of Islay	Seaweed/Iodine/Dry	Seaweed/Salty	A
5.	Ardmore	Speyside	Malty/Sherry	Fruity/Grain	A
6.	Arran	Isle of Arran	First malt planned for 2003		
7.	Auchentoshan	Lowlands	Lemon	Citronella	B and A
8.	Auchroisk	Speyside	Licorice/Malty	Licorice/Caramel	A
9.	Aultmore	Speyside	Cut grass/Dry	Floral/Fruity	B
10.	Balblair*	Northern Highlands	Fruity (Pear)	Spicy/Sherry	B
11.	Balmenach*	Speyside	Heather Honey	Sherry/Honey	A
12.	Balvenie	Speyside	Orange/Honey	Orange/Spicy	A
13.	Ben Nevis	Western Highlands	Floral/Smoky	Malty/Toffee	A
14.	Benriach	Speyside	Fruity/Floral	Malty/Floral	B
15.	Benrinnes	Speyside	Floral/Smoky	Dry/Toffee	B and A
16.	Benromach*	Speyside	Floral/Sherry	Woody/Malty	A
17.	Bladnoch*	Lowlands	Lemon/Grassy	Lemon/Red fruits	B and A
18.	Blair Athol	Southern Highlands	Spicy/Sherry	Ginger/Dry	B and A
19.	Bowmore	Isle of Islay	Smoky/Salty/Sherry	Licorice/Sherry	B and A
20.	Braes of Glenlivet	Speyside	Honey	Citrus	B
21.	Brora***	Northern Highlands	Peat	Walnut/Smoky	A
22.	Bruichladdich*	Isle of Islay	Malty/Salty	Seaweed/Dry/Salty	B
23.	Bunnahabhain	Isle of Islay	Floral/Iodine	Malty	B and A
24.	Caol Ila	Isle of Islay	Peat/Fruity	Peat/Spicy	B and A
25.	Caperdonich	Speyside	Smoky	Malty/Fruity/Spicy	B and A
26.	Cardhu	Speyside	Sweet	Sweet/Malty	B and A
27.	Clynelish	Northern Highlands	Salty/Peat	Malty/Seaweed/Salty	A
28.	Coleburn***	Speyside	Smoky/Dry	Malty/Smoky	B
29.	Convalmore***	Speyside	Sweet	Malty/Sweet	A
30.	Cragganmore	Speyside	Floral/Dry	Floral/Malty	A
31.	Craigellachie	Speyside	Sweet/Malty	Citrus/Sweet	A
32.	Dailuaine	Speyside	Sherry/Dry	Fruity/Vegetal/Dry	A
33.	Dallas Dhu**	Speyside	Malty/Peat	Malty/Toffee	A
34.	Dalmore	Northern Highlands	Citrus/Sherry	Sweet/Spicy/Malty	A
35.	Dalwhinnie	Speyside	Floral/Dry	Malty/Honey/Peat	B
36.	Deanston	Southern Highlands	Fresh	Dry	B and A
37.	Dufftown	Speyside	Smoky/Dry	Smoky/Dry	B
38.	Edradour	Southern Highlands	Spicy/Sherry	Spicy/Malty	A
39.	Fettercairn	Highlands	Hazelnut/Sherry	Sweet/Dry	B
40.	Glen Elgin	Speyside	Citrus/Honey	Citrus/Floral	B and A
41.	Glen Garioch*	Eastern Highlands	Heather/Peat	Sweet/Honey/Dry	B and A
42.	Glen Grant	Speyside	Floral/Dry	Fruity/Dry	B and A
43.	Glen Keith	Speyside	Woody/Spicy	Spicy/Sweet	B
44.	Glen Moray	Speyside	Sweet/Cut grass	Sweet/Malty	B
45.	Glen Ord	Northern Highlands	Malty/Dry/Peat	Malty/Dry	A
46.	Glen Scotia***	Campbeltown	Fresh/Salty	Malty/Dry/Salty	B and A
47.	Glen Spey	Speyside	Cut grass	Cut grass	B
48.	Glenallachie	Speyside	Sweet/Malt	Sweet	B
49.	Glenburgie-Glenlivet	Speyside	Wax	Orange/Dry	B
50.	Glencadam	Eastern Highlands	Fruity	Sweet/Malty	B and A
51.	Glendronach*	Speyside	Sweet/Oloroso Sherry	Sweet/Malty/Sherry	A
52.	Glendullan	Speyside	Fruity/Malty	Fruity/Malty/Dry	A
53.	Glenesk*	Eastern Highlands	Fresh	Malty/Dry	B
54.	Glenfarclas	Speyside	Woody/Sherry/Toffee	Fruity/Dry/Sherry	A

A N D   B L E N D S

*** Buildings in place but no longer functioning

	Distilleries	Region	Nose principal notes	Flavor principal notes	Before a meal (B) After a meal (A)
55.	Glenfiddich	Speyside	Fruity/Dry	Pear/Dry	B and A
56.	Glenglassaugh*	Speyside	Spicy/Grassy	Spicy/Fruity/Cut grass	B
57.	Glengoyne	Western Highlands	Malty/Dry/Sherry	Sweet/Fruity/Malty	B and A
58.	Glenkinchie	Lowlands	Cut grass	Sweet/Fresh/Dry	B and A
59.	Glenlivet	Speyside	Floral/Sherry	Floral/Fruity	B
60.	Glenlochy***	Western Highlands	Peat/Dry	Peat/Dry	A
61.	Glenlossie	Speyside	Grassy/Vegetal	Malty/Dry	B
62.	Glenmorangie	Western Highlands	Caramel/Toffee	Sweet/Caramel	B and A
63.	Glenrothes	Speyside	Sherry/Peat	Spicy/Dry/Peat	A
64.	Glentauchers	Speyside	Medicinal	Malty/Dry	B
65.	Glenturret	Southern Highlands	Malty/Sweet/Dry	Charred wood/Dry	B and A
66.	Glenury-Royal***	Eastern Highlands	Sherry/Dry	Sweet/Malty/Dry	B and A
67.	Highland Park	Orkneys	Heather/Smoky/Honey	Heather/Vegetal	B and A
68.	Imperial	Speyside	Sweet	Spicy/Sherry	A
69.	Inchgower	Speyside	Salty/Dry	Malty/Dry/Salty	B and A
70.	Inverleven*	Lowlands	Smoky/Cut grass	Citrus/Spicy	B and A
71.	Isle of Jura	Isle of Jura	Salty/Vegetal/Dry	Sweet/Floral	B
72.	Kininvie	Speyside	Floral/Dry	Dry	B
73.	Knockando	Speyside	Red fruits	Fruity/Sherry	B
74.	Knockdhu	Speyside	Fruity	Fruity/Walnut	A
75.	Lagavulin	Isle of Islay	Salty/Sherry/Peat	Smoky/Salty/Peat	B and A
76.	Laphroaig	Isle of Islay	Seaspray/Medicinal	Seaweed/Salty	A
77.	Linkwood	Speyside	Floral/Sherry	Almond	B and A
78.	Littlemill*	Lowlands	Sweet	Sweet/Malty	B and A
79.	Loch Lomond	Southern Highlands	Medicinal	Spicy	B and A
80.	Lochside***	Eastern Highlands	Floral	Red fruits	B
81.	Longmorn	Speyside	Floral/Malty	Malty/Fruity	B and A
82.	Macallan	Speyside	Spicy/Sherry	Oak/Walnut/Sherry	A
83.	Macduff	Eastern Highlands	Malty/Sherry	Malty	A
84.	Mannochmore*	Speyside	Floral	Fruity	B
85.	Miltonduff-Glenlivet	Speyside	Floral/Peat	Sweet/Floral	B
86.	Mortlach	Speyside	Malty/Sherry	Smoky/Sherry	A
87.	Oban	Western Highlands	Malty/Peat	Fruity/Smoky	A
88.	Pittyvaich*	Speyside	Pear	Williams pear	A
89.	Port Ellen***	Isle of Islay	Spicy/Salty	Pepper/Salty	A
90.	Pulteney	Northern Highlands	Salty	Salty/Sherry	B
91.	Rosebank*	Lowlands	Vegetal	Floral/Fruity	B
92.	Royal Brackla	Northern Highlands	Smoky	Spicy/Fruity	A
93.	Royal Lochnagar	Eastern Highlands	Spicy/Sherry	Spicy/Fruity/Malty	A
94.	Scapa*	Orkneys	Chocolate	Salty/Chocolate	B
95.	Speyburn	Speyside	Cut grass	Malty/Grassy	B
96.	Speyside	Northern Highlands	Floral/Peat	Sweet/Fruity	B
97.	Springbank	Campbeltown	Salty/Sherry/Peat	Smoky/Salty/Toffee	B and A
98.	Strathisla	Speyside	Woody/Malty	Oak/Sherry	A
99.	Strathmill	Speyside	Citrus	Honey/Citrus	B
100.	Talisker	Isle of Skye	Smoky/Seaweed/Salty	Smoky/Pepper	A
101.	Tamdhu	Speyside	Caramel	Malty/Caramel	B and A
102.	Tamnavulin*	Speyside	Cut grass	Red fruits	B
103.	Teaninich	Northern Highlands	Fruity	Spicy/Peat	B and A
104.	Tobermory	Isle of Mull	Mentholated	Spicy	B and A
105.	Tomatin	Speyside	Malty/Spicy	Caramel/Spicy	B and A
106.	Tomintoul	Speyside	Cut grass	Malty	B
107.	Tormore	Speyside	Almond	Malty/Almond	B and A
108.	Tullibardine*	Southern Highlands	Malty	Malty/Fruity	B

SELECT MALTS AND BLENDS

UNITED STATES

Distilleries	Brands	Nose principal notes	Flavor principal notes	Before a meal (B) After a meal (A)
Bourbons				
1. Ancient Age	Ancient Age	Vanilla/Orange	Spicy/Tobacco	A
	Benchmark	Vanilla	Citrus/Vanilla	B and A
	Eagle Rare	Caramel/Vanilla	Citrus/Tobacco	A
	Benchmark XO (single barrel)	Spicy/Vanilla	Cinnamon/Orange/Vanilla	A
	Blanton's (single barrel)	Orange/Honey/Vanilla	Spicy/Orange/Vanilla	A
	Elmer T. Lee (single barrel)	Woody/Fruity	Red fruits	A
	Hancock's Reserve (single barrel)	Caramel/Vanilla	Caramel/Cigar	A
2. Barton	Very Old Barton	Woody/Vanilla	Spicy	B and A
	Kentucky Gentleman	Woody/Spicy	Tobacco/Vanilla	B and A
	Ten High	Spicy/Vanilla	Caramel/Vanilla	B and A
	Colonel Lee	Caramel/Vanilla	Woody/Caramel	B and A
	Barclay's	Woody/Vanilla	Spicy	B and A
3. Jim Beam	Jim Beam	Cinnamon/Vanilla	Spicy/Fruity	B and A
	Old Taylor	Tobacco/Vanilla	Rye/Vanilla/Tobacco	A
	Old Crow	Citrus/Tobacco	Spicy	B
	Old Grand Dad	Honey/Rye	Woody/Spicy/Smoky	A
	Booker's (small batch)	Woody/Orange/Vanilla	Fruity/Tobacco	A
	Basil Hayden's (small batch)	Spicy/Vanillas	Citrus/Spicy	B
	Knob Creek (small batch)	Woody/Spicy/Honey	Citrus/Red fruits	A
	Baker's (small batch)	Citrus/Red fruits	Almond/Vanilla	B and A
	Old Overholt (rye)	Spicy/Fruity	Fruity/Rye	B and A
4. Bernheim	W.L. Weller	Caramel/Spicy/Honey	Caramel/Spicy/Honey	A
	I.W.Harper	Spicy/Fruity	Red fruits/Vanilla	A
	Old Charter	Spicy/Honey	Caramel/Honey/Vanilla	A
	Old Fitzgerald	Woody/Leather	Caramel/Leather/Tobacco	A
	Rebel Yell	Fruity/Honey	Spicy/Fruity/Honey	A
5. Early Times	Early Times	Honey/Vanilla	Leather/Tobacco	A
	Old Forester	Leather/Spicy/Vanilla	Citrus/Caramel/Spicy	A
6. Four Roses	Four Roses	Caramel/Mentholated	Caramel/Honey	B and A
7. Heaven Hill	Heaven Hill	Strawberry/Vanilla	Woody/Sweet	B and A
	Evan Williams	Woody/Vanilla	Caramel/Vanilla	B and A
	Elijah Craig	Citrus/Vanilla	Caramel/Vanilla	A
	Henry McKenna	Woody/Vanilla	Woody/Leather	B and A
	J.T.S. Brown	Woody/Vanilla	Woody	B and A
	J.W.Dant	Woody/Vanilla	Woody/Leather	B and A
8. Maker's Mark	Maker's Mark	Leather/Honey/Vanilla	Spicy/Fruity/Mentholated	A
9. Wild Turkey	Wild Turkey	Citrus/Honey/Vanilla	Citrus/Spicy/Vanilla	B and A
	Wild Turkey (single barrel)	Mentholated/Tobacco	Honey/Cigar	A
Tennessee whiskeys				
10. Jack Daniel	Jack Daniel's	Charred wood/Caramel	Spicy/Tobacco	B and A
	Gentleman Jack	Charred wood/Honey	Charred wood/Fruity	A
11. George A. Dickel	George A. Dickel	Charred wood/Toffee	Apple/Tobacco	B and A
Virginia whiskeys				
12. Smith Bowman	Virginia Gentleman	Mentholated/Honey	Honey/Vanilla	B and A

IRELAND

Distilleries	Brands	Nose principal notes	Flavor principal notes	Before a meal (B) After a meal (A)
Midleton	Jameson	Sherry/Sweet	Malty/Fruity	B
	Jameson Crested Ten	Spicy/Malty/Sherry	Spicy/Toffee	B
	Jameson 1780	Spicy/Sherry	Spicy/Sherry/Vanilla	B and A
	Midleton VR	Spicy/Honey/Sherry	Spicy/Malty	B and A
	Paddy	Grain/Fruity	Grain/Bitter	B
	Power's	Grain/Spicy/Vanilla	Spicy/Honey	B and A
	Redbreast	Red fruits/Sherry	Spicy/Malty/Honey	A
	Tullamore Dew	Malty	Spicy/Vanilla	B
	Green Spot	Woody/Malty/Sherry	Spicy/Malty/Sweet	B and A
Bushmills	Bushmills Original	Grain/Sherry	Sweet	B
	Bushmills Black Bush	Grain/Sherry	Spicy/Malty/Sherry	B and A
	Bushmills Malt	Malty/Sherry	Malty/Sherry/Sweet	B and A
	Coleraine	Grain/Sweet	Woody/Grain	B
Cooley	Kilbeggan	Fruity/Sweet	Sweet	B
	John Locke	Malty/Sweet	Malty/Honey	B
	Tyrconnel	Spicy/Fruity/Honey	Citrus/Honey	B and A
	Connemara	Sherry	Smoky/Malty	B and A

JAPAN

Distilleries	Brands	Nose principal notes	Flavor principal notes	Before a meal (B) After a meal (A)
Yamazaki	Yamazaki	Malty	Malty/Sweet	B
Yoichi	Hokkaido	Malty/Dry	Smoky/Sherry	B and A
Karuizawa	Karuizawa	Woody/Sherry	Malty/Sherry	B
Gotemba	Crescent	Woody/Dry	Smoky/Dry	B

SCOTLAND AND CANADA (BLENDS)

Family	Brands	Nose principal notes	Flavor principal notes	Before a meal (B) After a meal (A)
Scottish	Ballantine's Finest	Spicy/Fruity	Spicy/Vanilla	B
	Black & White	Sweet	Cut grass/Sweet	B
	Chivas Regal	Smoky/Malty/Sweet	Malty/Sweet	B and A
	Cutty Sark	Very dry	Sweet	B
	Dewar's White Label	Smoky/Malty	Malty/Dry	B
	J&B Rare	Cut Grass/Dry	Vegetal/Dry	B
	Johnnie Walker Red Label	Fruity/Smoky	Fruity/Dry	B
	The Famous Grouse	Woody/Caramel	Woody/Sweet	B
	Vat 69	Smoky/Malty	Smoky/Malty	B
	White Horse	Spicy/Dry	Smoky/Dry	B
	Dimple	Sweet/Smoky	Sweet/Peat	B
Canadian	Canadian Club	Dry	Fruity/Rye	B
	Crown Royal	Smoky	Woody/Rye	B
	Schenley OFC	Rye/Dry	Sweet/Rye	B

I N D E X

SELECTED BIBLIOGRAPHY

Arthur, Helen. *Whisky: The Water of Life*. Westport, CT: Firefly, 2000.

Behr, Edward. *Prohibition: Thirteen Years That Changed America*. New York: Arcade, 1997.

Hills, Phillip. *Appreciating Whisky*. Pomfret, VT: Trafalgar Square, 2000.

Hume, John Robert. *The Making of Scotch Whisky*. Edinburgh: Canongate, 2000.

Lamond, John, and Robin Tucek. *The Malt Whisky File*. New York: Lyons Press, 1998.

Regan, Gary. *The Book of Bourbon and Other Fine American Whiskeys*. Boston: Houghton Mifflin, 1995.

Shaw, Carol P. *Whisky*. Glasgow: HarperCollins, 1999.

Photographic credits: Chivas Glenlivet Group 55; United Distillers 78, 54; EDINBURGH, National Gallery of Scotland 81; LONDON, Bridgeman 16–17, 36, 74, 105; NEW YORK, Bettmann Archive 32, 112; PADUA, Museo Civico 87 bottom; PARIS, Archives Photos 24–25, 28, 33, 47, 94, 71, 73; Jacques Boulay 78, 61; Olivier Beytout 93; Jean-Loup Charmet 31, 70; Dagli Orti 14, 26, 43, 98; Magnum/Michael K. Nichols 30, 97 top /F. Scianna 49, 50, 53 /George Rodger 4–5, 51, 102/Ian Berry 75 /Elliott Erwitt 85; Maison du Whisky/Guérard cover, 38, 56, 60, 63, 62, 66, 79, 103 top; Erwan Quéméré 10, 18–19, 42, 44, 45, 110–111, 90–91, 52, 53, 40, 59, 64, 69, 75, 95, 96, 80, 100–101, 54, 29; Roger Viollet 39, 86–87; Scope/Philipp Gould 34, 106, 76, 82–83 /D. Faure 41; VANVES, Explorer/B. Gérard 20–21, 23 /E. Brenckle 38 bottom, 72 /Manix 56–57; Giraudon/Alinari 46 © ADAGP 1996 /Bridgeman 89.

Translated from the French by Robert Orchard and Susan Pickford
Adaptation and additional research by Kathryn Lancaster
Copy-editing: Gillian Delaforce
Typesetting: Julie Houis, À Propos
Color separation: Pollina S.A., France

ISBN: 2-08010-626-0
N° d'édition: FA0626-01-VII
Dépôt légal: 10/2001
Printed and bound by Pollina S.A., France - n° L84360